A FLICKER IN THE WATER

Inside the Tales

BOB GONZALEZ

A Flicker in the Water
Copyright © 2022 by Bob Gonzalez. All rights reserved.

No part of this book may be used or reproduced in any manner whatsoever without written permission, except in the case of brief quotations embodied in critical articles and reviews. For more information, e-mail all inquiries to info@mindstirmedia.com.

Published by Mindstir Media, LLC
45 Lafayette Rd | Suite 181| North Hampton, NH 03862 | USA
1.800.767.0531 | www.mindstirmedia.com

Printed in the United States of America

ISBN-13: 979-8-9862953-8-1 (paperback)

Every sea adventure starts at the shoreline. Raft along with us, as we go for an exciting sea journey "Inside the Tales" of "A FLICKER IN THE WATER" BY: BOB GONZALEZ

A FLICKER IN THE WATER

Foreword

Having grown up in a family that loved to fish this book spoke to me at a deep level of appreciation. My father, the first son of world-renowned author Ernest Hemingway has a story of fishing from his childhood that I knew well because my father Jack Hemingway made it known that this story, which I am about to tell you, is the reason he fished nearly every day of his life, when he finally came of age and when was *allowed* to fish.

Let me explain…my father was raised the first 10 years of his life in Paris France and his father left him and my grandmother Hadley when he was only 2 years old. But Papa, as Ernest was called, visited my dad annually as a child and took him to the fishing streams and beaches that he loved the most. The interesting thing is that when he visited my dad he took, Bumby (my dad's most embarrassing knick name, according to dad) fishing, only Papa fished…he wouldn't allow his son to do anything but watch. For years my father watched his dad fly fish, and deep-sea fish off the deck of the Pilar, which he acquired when he moved to Cuba and when my father visited him there. But until he was around 16 or 17 he was only allowed to watch his father fish. As you can imagine a boy yearning to learn and become good at something, those years of *watching* created a desire to fish in my dad that couldn't be satiated right up to the end of his life. My dad's *watching* spawned (pun intended) a deep understanding of the water (whether fresh or salt water) and a true understanding of the fish and what they wanted to eat and at what time of the day they wanted it. My dad became a world-renowned fisherman. He fished around the world and fished most days of his life even when I was growing up in a small town in Idaho.

Fishing, as my dad taught me over the years and his father taught him is more about the experience, the water, the fresh air, the temperature, the stillness or the current and of course the landscape or seascape that surrounds you, than it is about hauling fish onto the deck. There is a zen to fishing that speaks only to those that have gone out into the water and experienced everything about the environment they are in. You are a visitor when you are out in the ocean, it is a world you must respect and honor as far more powerful than any man. The sea belongs and is run by the creatures that live and survive there.

Bob Gonzalez's book is an homage to fisherman and their need to explore the water especially when deep-sea fishing. It is a sport of course but for the fisherman, it is a religion. So bravo to Bob Gonzalez for this poignant window into the world of the deep sea and the extraordinary fish that call it home. **A Flicker in the Water** is a telling title to the stories that emerge from that flicker. I tip my hat to Bob Gonzalez, to my dad and to my grandfather who also see/saw the flickers of the water as a symbol of the men they wanted to be, men who spoke the language of the water.

Mariel Hemingway

A FLICKER IN THE WATER

Inside the Tales

The water was brightly lit, reflecting the Tuna's iridescent colors off of their elongated muscular bodies as we arrived at sunset. Getting to the offshore oil rigs, our fishing destination had been no easy journey. An eight-hour trek through an unpredictable yet calm sea. On the way we had managed to land a bull dolphin. In Spanish they are called dorado. An apt name that perfectly captures the golden essence of their beautiful multicolored skin tone with differing vibrant shades of blue, green and striking yellow capped off by a flat squared bulging head creating a color combination as diverse and beautiful as any fish in the sea. Most know them as mahi -mahi, a Hawaiian term that means "very strong." The bull, a male had a companion with him, a female called a cow. Male lions are the kings of the jungle, but in the world's oceans females wear the crown, reigning supreme. Captain Mike had made the trip many times before, but even an experienced seaman cannot help getting those little butterflies in the pit of his stomach as the departure time draws closer. The excited anticipation of what could happen good or bad when leaving the dock is a different-yet-no-less-satisfying feeling than a successful trip's return. Filling the coolers with ice, rigging bait, setting the rods and reels to the proper length and drag are all necessary tasks to be done ahead of time, because as any fisherman knows you want to be ready when you get that make-or-break strike. Which as every fisherman who has ever told tales also knows happens each time you put your baits in the water. Doing these required tasks for the Twister's crew team would be Troby (known as Drawbridge to his friends). Drawbridge was an experienced fisherman who had more stories to tell than Popeye the sailor man, only he did not derive his strength from spinach. Drawbridge was a jovial fellow with the look of an experienced fisherman written on the lines of his face, who like many seamen had an unquenchable thirst for the suds, which often led to some amusing and at times not-so-amusing circumstances. There was never a bridge Drawbridge did not want to cross or a fish he didn't like to eat (once comparing the taste of a tiger shark's liver to a chocolate bar). Drawbridge's father had been an airline pilot for a major airline, before becoming an early settler in Destin while it was still known as the "World's Luckiest Fishing Village." Drawbridge spent a lot of his childhood traveling the world through the air. Choosing for himself as an adult to travel by water. Also joining the crew was Gary, a local kid who had grown up fishing the local waters. Bob Jr. a former ballplayer who enjoyed all aspects of the seaman's experience from preparation to scrubbing the boat down after a long run. Bob Jr.'s favorite baseball memory was of a home run he hit in a championship game. "I still don't know how that ball traveled so far. It felt like the ball slipped off the bat, it must have gotten caught up in a favorable wind current." In baseball like at sea it's better traveling when the currents are in your favor.

Bob Jr. hailed from the mountains of Northeast Pennsylvania. He and Bob Sr. fished for bluefish off the coast of New Jersey every summer. Bob Jr. likes to retell the story that brought him of age as a fisherman, the first Bluefish he reeled in by himself at age nine. The warrior in him came alive, refusing to hand the rod off. "It was going to be the fish or me," he likes to say. Bob Jr. had taken a renewed special interest not wanting to call it outright pride in his gaffing. Line up the gaff to the fish then give it a quick short snatch instead of lunging at the fish. He would say, "You won't get them all but your batting average will definitely improve. His love of gaffing was born out of a near miss of a 100lb. wahoo that had somehow managed to slip off the hook after repeated gaff attempts (by others), the shockwaves of which felt like a harpoon had lodged itself in his heart, needing to be carefully removed. Bob Sr. was the boat's principal owner. Bob Sr. is not your typical sit in the chair, content to reel in the fish kind of a boat owner. Bob Sr. likes to get his hands dirty with everyone else. He once caught a giant albacore tuna off the shores of Barnegat Light New Jersey on an old party boat called "Doris Mae" that won him the day's pool prize. The pool prize was a potluck all the day's fishermen contributed to before heading out for the day. Barnegat Light was known for their catches of bluefish in the summer and cod in winter. Bob Sr. had been on such a hot streak of late. He caught a 42 lb. red snapper three pounds shy of the Florida state record and a 60 lb. grouper all within ten minutes of each other. Having grown up in Cuba, Bob Sr. spent much of his childhood on the ocean; he learned how to swim before he could walk. In the tradition of fishermen of that day he started fishing with an old school hand line. The crusty fishermen, many of whom made their living with their hand lines developed hands so calloused they felt like sandpaper to the touch. But their hands were really tender when it came to working a fish. As a ten year old in Santiago de Cuba, Bob Sr. caught his first fish on a hand line, a tarpon who at the time weighed as much as he did 80 lbs. within view of the EL Morro Castle, the stately looking fort sitting at the mouth of "La Bahia de Santiago." Bob Sr. put a rope through the fish's gills, threw the fish over his shoulder, the fish's tail dragging on the ground behind him. The experience would come in handy (literally) years later when he had a three-sided treble hook get stuck in his finger when he brought a kicking bull mahi on board. Each time the mahi kicked the treble lodged itself deeper and deeper. After subduing the fish, we used a wire cutter to slice the steel hook pulling it out of his finger. Bob Sr. didn't flinch. We bandaged his finger, applied some ointment with a dose of hydrogen peroxide, and continued fishing without skipping a beat. Little did Bob Sr. know his recent hot streak was about to continue. This was no ordinary bottom fishing trip they were embarking on. No, sir, this time around they were after one of the sea's toughest competitors. Tuna are known as being finicky feeders, and on this day they lived up to their well deserved reputation. Arriving at dusk you could see their stout bodies protruding from the water in a way that said, "yeah, we know you're here. Now see if you can catch us." Tuna are so unpredictable many times they don't even let you approach them without going under water, losing themselves in the depths without a trace to be seen. There hasn't been a depth finder made yet they haven't been able to outrun. To catch them, we tried, then tried, then tried again. Nine long hours had passed since the tuna began teasing us. Up to now they were winning the battle of wills in the depths of the 5,000 feet we were fishing. They gave us no indication that they were even still around, seeming to have disappeared. In the interim a few cases of beer, which would have tasted much better with some freshly caught raw tuna fish as a side dish, had been consumed. Innate in the fishermen's nature is the pleasure of believing the fish always tastes better when it's caught with his own hand, the pursuit accomplished.

Drawbridge had on a past voyage had a harrowing experience with a boatload of beer. Drawbridge was commissioned with delivery of a vessel from Destin Florida to Cabo San Lucas in Baja, California, where he and his team were going to fish in a marlin tournament. In years gone by Drawbridge had won first prize in this tournament, leading the pack weighing in a grander blue marlin. The boat's owner was a builder who built condominiums all along the Gulf coast. Drawbridge was always proud, not boastful, just proud the winning grander he landed was measured by girth and length being hung in the entrance way of the first condo his boss built. He could be heard saying from time to time, "Oh yeah, when my dad helped settle Holiday Isle, he never dreamed his son would leave a lasting legacy to carry on his family name." On this current excursion things would take on a decidedly different twist. No one really knows how or why, but legend has it the boat Drawbridge commandeered was loaded with cases of beer from bow to stern with only enough space to walk from the bridge to the bathroom through a narrow aisle down below. He and his girlfriend Gail set sail in what was thought to be balmy, ideal conditions, feet up enjoying a brand new day's sunrise. As is often the case, Mother Nature makes plans of her own on short notice, rarely if ever consulting anyone about them. Crossing the Florida Straits at nightfall can be delightful with a following sea allowing tired hard working engines a temporary reprieve. The vast current propelling the boat forward. Going against those same currents can often be a challenging if not downright horrifying experience, as Drawbridge and Gail would soon find out.

BOB GONZALEZ

EL Morro Castle overlooking the bay of Santiago de Cuba. Santiago was once the capital city of Cuba. The fort was built to protect the city from pirates in the 1600s. Today it is used as a museum, culminating each day at sunset with a ceremonial firing of the cannon. This is where Bob Sr. caught his first tarpon with an old fashioned hand line.

A FLICKER IN THE WATER

The view overlooking Santiago de Cuba from atop from El Morro Castle. According to UNESCO, it is the best preserved and most complete example of Spanish-American military architecture. The view is not too shabby either!

Bob Jr. displaying his gaffing skills. He was able to get this one through the mouth, saving all the wahoo's tasty meat in the process.

A FLICKER IN THE WATER

Bob Sr. with a bull dolphin caught on the way to the Louisiana oil rigs.

BOB GONZALEZ

Drawbridge on the top photo ready to drop down a bait.
Bottom photo is a marlin he helped catch, then released.

FLICKER IN THE WATER

Part 2

Realizing as the hour turned to 3AM sunrise was only two short hours away, we tied the boat to a supply buoy," shutting off her engines figuring it was time to try another method of fishing. Instead of dragging lures around, we tried jigging artificial baits called spoons up and down the water column. Having a varied selection of live baits kept fresh in the live well as backups to be used if needed. Having a well functioning livewell pumping water through the baitfish, giving their gills much-needed oxygen in the confined space keeps the bait fresh and lively. There can never be enough fresh live bait onboard for a fishing trip. Fresh live bait can be the difference between an ordinary trip or possibly catching the fish of a lifetime. Jigging is a lot like playing tug of war with the water. A couple of pulls on the line followed by a couple of cranks of the reel. The water resistance provides a better workout for your arms and shoulders than lifting any free weights ever could. Fastened at the end of the line was a long silvery precious metal in the shape of a banana. The light from the oil rigs was reflected by the silver jig, which in turn we hoped a flicker of would catch the fish's eye. When live baiting, the bait does the work for you, dancing around in the water trying to get the fish's attention. The more seductive the dance, the better. Live baits also give off a natural vibration exuding a scent trail in the water that an artificial lure simply can not, no matter how you dress it up. The middle-of-the-night air smelled of sea salt that could clear anyone's sinuses. And the sweat from the summertime humidity which was thicker than a bowl of clam chowder could cause a salty tear to melt in your eye. Life at sea always agreed with me. A real fisherman can be landlocked for only so long before the itch of chasing that fish needs scratching. It's the battle between man and beast that keeps the motor burning in your psyche, and if you are lucky enough fuel in your boat's engines to keep going those extra miles.

A FLICKER IN THE WATER

Destin Florida's East Pass. Our home port, the only gateway to the Gulf of Mexico, 50 miles west of Panama City and 50 miles east of Pensacola.

BOB GONZALEZ

One of over 200 oil rigs found off the coast of Louisiana. The Gulf of Mexico is one of the most important offshore petroleum-production regions in the world, accounting for 1/6th of the energy production for the USA. World class big game fishing is an added bonus.

A FLICKER IN THE WATER

The mouth of the East Pass, Destin, Florida, the jewel of the Emerald coast.
The water clarity here is unsurpassed anywhere else in Florida.

FLICKER IN THE WATER

Part 3

We had turned our engines off earlier in the evening at sundown, not believing we would need them again until sunrise the following morning. Now in the middle of the night with only the sound of the boat generator audible. The thought of getting any sleep was not on anyone's mind. The light chop of the water mimicking the feeling of a baby's crib being rocked would provide enough relaxation as we continued to pursue our prize. In fishing there are no lullabies, only alibis for the big one that always seems to get away in the last precious seconds of the battle. Anyone who has ever thrown a bait in the water knows the feeling. The pain lasts longer than years on a lunar calendar and never really leaves the fiber of your being. It only grows larger with the passage of time, but it builds character making you a better person. Being a better fisherman is a byproduct of what might have been. After all, whether a fish is caught or not is never really up to the fisherman. The fisherman does all he can to make it happen. After that it's left to the creator who created the fishes in the sea and the birds in the sky on the fifth day, man and land animals coming on the sixth. Before resting on the seventh. 950 yards of monofilament line at

80lb test were spooled onto our heavy duty reels. More than a full season of yards gained for the best of professional football players. At a standstill with no drag on the reel, a big yellowfin tuna would snap 80lb of test force line like a person stepping on a twig in the forest. The reel gives the line the back and forth similar to the action of a rubber band. Oil rigs are fertile fishing grounds off the coast of Louisiana. It keeps fish warm in the winter months, providing them structure to protect themselves from larger predators. It's not unheard of for a big blue marlin, a swordfish, or worse yet large sharks of all kinds, bull, tiger, mako, blacktip, hammerhead, or the fiercest of all, the Jaws of the misunderstood great white to traverse these waters in search of easy prey. Great whites were believed to not inhabit the Gulf of Mexico. Old folklore mistakenly thought the water was not cold enough for them. That myth has been unwound with many sightings in recent years. The great white caught off the pier in Navarre dispelled the notion forever. For our purposes and for the tuna we were chasing, the rigs provided light from their platforms, illuminating the oceans waves reflecting the water with light giving it a vibrant lively feeling of a city that never sleeps. Only New Yorkers would truly understand. The importance of the Gulf of Mexico as an energy producer can not be minimized accounting for one sixth of the petroleum produced for the U.S. There are over 200 oil rigs or so off the Louisiana coast alone. I like to refer to them as underwater skyscrapers. Some of them only go down as shallow as thirty feet, while others like the one we fished sink into the depths to 5,000 feet or deeper. One of them, the infamous deep water rig Horizon as it's known does its drilling in this area also, tapping the oil from the Gulf's bottom at down under 5,000 feet. A story about fishing the oil rigs of the northern Gulf of Mexico would be incomplete without mentioning the Horizon oil spill of 2010. After much consternation, the initial shock of the spill's aftermath took a few years to subside. But subside it did, like an outgoing tide, washing all its fears away with it. Fears of losing the Gulf of Mexico forever including all its habitat has been put to rest. Many more years of research has shown the natural healing properties of the ocean have no man-made equal. The waters have recovered seemingly as of today with hardly a trace of the oil spill's effects.

We fished the area long before 2010. The tuna we were after would not have suffered any ill effects emanating from the spill. On an excursion like ours, every person has a specific assignment: the best fisherman work together as a team. Every assignment is as important as the other. One mistake at the wrong time could be the difference between exuberant exaltation or a lifetime of memories of the lunar moons. Maybe that's why it's called sportfishing. On the bridge at the helm was captain Mike. Mike was an experienced hand. He had been a first mate for many years and knew how to tie more knots on a fishing line in a way that not even the great Houdini could escape from. The captain's job is to steer the boat properly when the fish first strikes. A good captain knows when to back down (go in reverse) on a fish or throttle forward depending on the fish's pull, always being aware of the fish's swimming direction. It could be toward you, away from you, or sometimes straight down. Straight down is called sounding. A fish will usually sound when he knows he doesn't have much left in the fight as a last ditch effort. A lot of times a billfish will bury his bill into the ocean floor in an act that is not fully understood as being an act of defiance or surrender. Gary, Drawbridge, Bob Sr. & Bob Jr. alternated turns with rods in their hands. Our duties were interchangeable. If any of us got that bite we were looking for, we would instantly turn from fisherman to doorman to gaffman. Bob Sr. who had been hotter than a firecracker on the 4th of July once again had lady liberty smiling on the palm of his hand.

Replica of the 42 Lb. red snapper Bob Sr. caught. Just three pounds shy of the Florida state record. I've seen plenty of fishermen with a beer belly—this is the first snapper I have seen with one.

A FLICKER IN THE WATER

Hanging back at the dock, on the left, a Yellowfin tuna, the inspiration for "A FLICKER IN THE WATER." On the right a bull shark.

ANYONE WANT A BEER

As Drawbridge approached the Florida Straits, the area that extends between Key West and Cuba also known as part of the famed Devil's triangle, the seas glistened like a sheet of glass or "slick as a baby's rear" as Captain Mike used to like to say. In the blink of an eye turned from calm cobalt blue to huge crested purple swells churning up foamy white edges at the top of its crested tips. A sudden summer thunderstorm carrying accompanying gale-force winds with it engulfed his boat, named "Carpe Diem." Gale-force winds usually call for a "small craft advisory," a warning for vessels 60 ft or less in length to stay in port. Unfortunately for Drawbridge this warning came in too late. Cropping up faster than an unnoticed giant bed of kelp forest to navigate through. Drawbridge now had two Gail's in his midst. One he needed to protect; the other he prayed went away as fast as it came! Drawbridge and his Gail began to wonder if indeed they would be "living for the day," or more aptly stated dying by the dead of night. Realizing the gravity of the situation, Drawbridge told Gail to seek shelter away from the storm down below while he radioed the coast guard for help. The captain's first responsibility is to look out for his crew first whatever the circumstances may be, ultimately going down with the ship if necessary. Drawbridge could not keep an eye on Gail while maintaining radio contact with the coast guard. He needed all his focus on the dire situation at hand. The coast guard is always there to help any vessel in distress. The problem was that the gulf stream currents had so forcefully pulled the "Carpe Diem" off course she was now in Cuban territorial waters, where the U.S. coast guard did not have any authority to carry out rescue operations. Frightened but undeterred, Drawbridge was determined to steer the ship through, knowing these storms though ferocious at times do not last forever. He wanted to go downstairs to check on Gail, who had not reemerged for several hours since going down below to seek refuge. He feared for the worst but could not pull himself away from the helm; he had to keep the boat steered bow into the waves. If the boat got turned, taking the impact of the waves on its side, the result could have been catastrophic. The coast guard told him they would monitor his whereabouts, keeping a log of his coordinates. It was somewhat of a consolation, but he knew it was up to him to "seize the day" if they were to survive. The 65 foot Carpe Diem, though not technically a "small craft," bobbed up and down thrown around like a cork floating in the ocean waves being lifted then dropped free fall with every wave toward the ocean bottom nonstop through the dark of night. Drawbridge's seaman skills were being put to the test. The storm left no time for self reflection. The time for soul searching would be coming soon enough. Finally after several hours, which felt like nine lifetimes, the seas again began to calm as daybreak began. In the Caribbean sea there is a renewal in energy that a sunrise on the ocean can only bring that can not be duplicated on land. Maybe it's God's promise of a brand new day. Wiping the slate clean brings a brand new purpose to set your sail toward. Maybe it's the combined silence of the waves with the solitude accompanied only by the echoed sounds of seagulls being audible. That allows the sun's rays to be fully absorbed. Whatever it was, Drawbridge was so excited for the first time in twelve hours to be able to check on Gail. It was a nervous excitement though not yet a relieved one. As he made his way below, his mind was racing, unsure of what he might find (if anything at all). Too pumped full of the adrenaline still running through his body not yet feeling the exhaustion that would come later, All the what if's crept in racing through his mind. What if on the way downstairs she had been thrown overboard…What if she banged her head knocking herself unconscious or worse? What if…..How will I be able to live with this guilt the rest of my life!! He asked himself. Thank God when Drawbridge looked inside the door Gail was OK. Good fortune had swung the bathroom door locked shut behind Gail, and she could not get up from her position to go out. With a mixture of tears of joy, relief, and possibly a touch of sadness, she jumped into Drawbridge's arms, vowing never to let go. With a promise from him to never go out to sea again without her. Now safely back in international waters, Drawbridge and Gail made their way to the nearest port on their radar Cancun, Mexico, where they would refuel and recharge their batteries before continuing south around through the Panama Canal. Drawbridge's fear of the ordeal he had just been through turned to excitement as he now would be able to tell his story of heroism to all the locals in Mexico. The beer he had on board was called Sol, meaning sun in Spanish. Drawbridge thought what a great story about the sun coming out to tell. What a better way to celebrate a renewed lease on life than with sun beer. What Drawbridge did not anticipate was the local authorities in Cancun were more interested in confiscating all the beer he had on board rather then listening to his stories of high seas adventure, which they were already all too familiar with.

This is what it looked like as Drawbrige and Gail departed toward Cabo San Lucas. A beautiful sunset, winds blowing at 5 to 10 knots with a light chop.

A FLICKER IN THE WATER

A few hours into the trip the Gulf still looks relaxed. The calm before the storm.

BOB GONZALEZ

Drawbridge, determined and steely eyed through his long night at the helm of the "Carpe Diem," had to have been just as focused as this sailor.

A FLICKER IN THE WATER

In the early evening the southern Gulf of Mexico was beginning to make its presence known.

Ominous sky. A sign of things to come.

A dangerous nightfall was only a short time away.

BOB GONZALEZ

Now the situation was dire. There are over three million shipwrecks around the world's oceans. Drawbridge was determined not to become one of them!

A FLICKER IN THE WATER

Sailors of all kinds, merchant seamen, explorers, and pirates have been caught up unexpectedly in rough treacherous seas for centuries.

BOB GONZALEZ

After a long scary night at sea, at sunrise the seas began to calm, for Drawbridge and Gail the promise of a new day never looked so good.

A FLICKER IN THE WATER

Drawbridge and Gail survived their ordeal, living to tell about it. God is good.

The unexpected night storm behind them, Drawbridge and Gail made their way to the closest port. Cancun, Mexico.

A FLICKER IN THE WATER

After the storm comes the rainbow. Rainbows have been a part of literature and culture for centuries with differing cultures applying their own meanings. For Drawbrige and Gail the rainbow's colors never shined so bright. Photo courtesy of Fishmonster Key West.

FLICKER IN THE WATER

Part 4

All of a sudden you could hear the reel screech. The rod Bob Sr. was holding was off to the races, or, more accurately, the depths. The live bait had worked like a charm, fitting perfectly into the tuna's hungry mouth, not slowing him down for an instant. The heat friction created by the drag on the line required pouring water on it and fast so it would not burn, melting the line. We all looked at each other in astonishment. All of us had caught Tuna before but none of us had ever seen an initial burst like this one. Seven hundred yards of line taken out and counting with no sign of letting up. We had to act fast or the fish would be going home with the brand new reel Drawbridge bought for Christmas. It never ceases to amaze how in the blink of an eye or in this case a bite out of nowhere can turn middle of the night doldrums into an adrenaline-filled high only a teenager with his first crush could experience. In the nick of time just before running out of line, we fastened another line with an even heavier duty reel to the original one then threw it in the water. Then in an unusual though not unprecedented move because of the extraordinary bite, we untied the boat from its mooring on the supply buoy, revving the engines up again to re-enter the battle. It was by the best of planning that we brought along two extra bladders for a little extra diesel fuel in case an unforeseen situation should arise. Bye bye, we waved at Drawbridge's reel, not knowing if we would ever be able to retrieve it or not. No matter how good or experienced a fisherman, the fish always has some say in these duels. On the new heavier duty reel the run continued unabated; we were not sure if we had a giant tuna on the line or next of kin to the fabled white whale Moby Dick. Right at the very moment when it began to look like we would be spooled again, the reel came to a sudden halt. The run was over. THANKFULLY. We were still far away from landing the fish, with a lot of work left to do. But at least now we would have a fighter's chance. Having taken 2,000 yards of line on the mighty run from us. That translates to a little bit over one mile of line that now had to be retrieved. The fish still had the upper hand. Until safely brought aboard, the fish always has the advantage. The battle is still being waged on his turf. In sports it's called home-field advantage. On the ocean we called it nature's advantage. More fish are lost right at the side of the boat than any other time. In that one mile any one of a number of things could have happened allowing the fish to live to fight another day. The amount of water pressure from the current puts a lot of stress on the line where it could snap at any moment. An unwanted entry into the fray from a large shark or a group of sharks could have ended the skirmish with one bite on the hooked fish. And has happened to any fisherman more than once. Recently Bob Jr. had a 60lb. monster bull dolphin that was about to be landed when suddenly it was devoured by a shark. Luckily the shark happened to bite the dolphin right in its midsection taking only the fish's organs with it. We liked to say the shark got its protein and we got our trophy allowing the fish to come on board with all its edible meat intact…. The tuna's mouth, once embedded in the hook, could be shaken off at any moment. Now it became our turn to have a say in landing this great fish that now, because of its uniqueness, we all felt connected to in ways that defy an ordinary tug on your line. Tuna, unlike mahi or marlin, will make a strong run but unlike mahi or marlin will not jump out of the water with sudden furious leaps, which sometimes resemble giant missiles coming up from the depths. Gary likes to tell a story about a wahoo that shot up through the water as if fired out of a cannon over the bow of the boat through the bridge window landing in the first mate's chair. The captain was so startled he jumped out of his chair yelling "wahoo!" Nobody was really sure if he was jumping for joy or frightened out of his chair....We began to slowly reel the fish back in, wanting to leave just enough tension on the line for the hook not to loosen up from the fish's mouth and just enough slack to not pull it out of the fish's mouth inadvertently. Crank after crank after crank the big battle turned into a kind of tug of war. We would gain some line, then the fish would make another run. Not as long or powerful as the initial run but enough to keep this back and forth going on for several more hours. Hour after hour with a focus so intense, making the hours feel like seconds, the runs kept getting just a bit shorter until we could see the outline of Drawbridges reel we had thrown in the water. Bob Sr. still holding the reel in his hands had to constantly have buckets of water poured over his head to keep from overheating and heavy doses of drinking water on hand to stay hydrated. In summer a fisherman could easily lose 10 lbs of bodily fluids, making dehydration a real possibility without ever noticing his focus being zoned in on the fish. As hot as the streak Bob Sr. had been on recently, he was the right person to be battling this fish. Now in his mid-sixties, he carried more energy than most fishermen half his age, having proven himself in his younger days as a high school senior at a military academy in Virginia, winning an ironman competition, and then years later achieving the rank of black belt in Tang Soo Do, a Korean form of martial arts. As spirited as these accomplishments were, Bob Sr. saved his most audacious undertaking when immediately after a long arduous fishing trip to Key West he drove nonstop to New York City, only stopping for gas. He would wake up before the seagulls. We would say if the boat's generator ever went down (which did happen on occasion), we could replace it with Bob's Sr.'s energy. A big victory was achieved when Drawbridge's reel came back to us. For one thing we were off the hook in having to pony up to buy him a new one. More importantly now for the first time since the fish's initial violent burst, the fish had allowed us to be on equal terms with him. One rod, one fish. Which meant we had closed the distance to half a mile.

BOB GONZALEZ

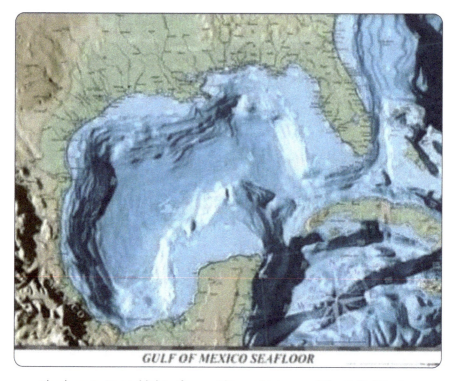

GULF OF MEXICO SEAFLOOR

Thank you to Port publishing for providing us this image of The Gulf of Mexico bottom contour. Notice how close to shore the continental shelf drops along the western part of the Gulf. These deep water drop-offs are some of the most fertile fishing grounds in the world. They extend from the western Florida panhandle to the Yucatan peninsula, where the deepest part of the Gulf called the Sigsbee deep is (13,000 feet). Big game paradise! The west coast of Florida is not as blessed with deep water so close to shore. The drop-off occurs approximately 100 miles from land. It was in the southwest area of Florida, exactly 98 miles from the shoreline, where our friend Mike witnessed the Florida state record yellowtail snapper caught.

A FLICKER IN THE WATER

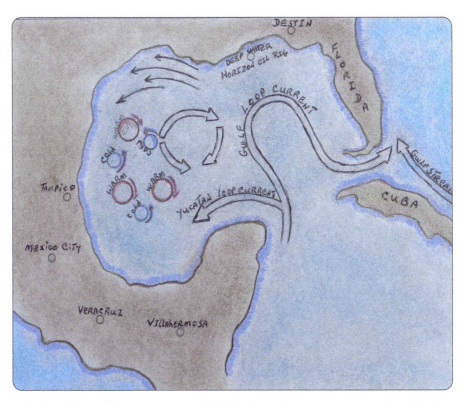

This hand-drawn illustration courtesy of Bob Sr. shows the continuous currents that flow in and out of the Gulf of Mexico. Even though the Gulf of Mexico, due to being landlocked, does not have drastic high or low tides, it is far from being a static body of water. The loop current and the offshoots it produces called eddies continually refresh the Gulf. The loop current is a warm water current that flows northward into the Gulf from the Caribbean south of the Yucatan Peninsula; it is one of the fastest moving currents in the Atlantic moving at approximately 5.6 mph. and is anywhere between 125 & 190 miles wide and 2,600 feet deep. The current sometimes barely extends into the Gulf while other times extending all the way to the northern Gulf coast of Florida and Louisiana before moving southeastward through the Florida Straits joining the Gulf Stream in the Atlantic. The circles in the drawing show the eddies, which randomly (every 3 to 17 months) break off from the loop current drifting westward at 5 mph. toward Texas and Mexico. The warm water eddies move in a clockwise motion while the cold water eddies move counterclockwise, lasting for about a year.

43

BOB GONZALEZ

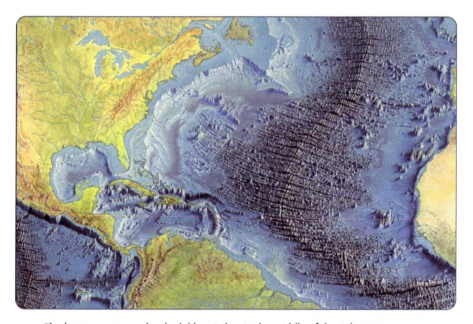

The bottom contours that look like stitches in the middle of the Atlantic ocean are actually underwater mountain ranges that connect to all the other oceans of the world. They wrap around the world extending over 40,000 miles (almost two times around the earth). A lot is still unknown about how it all ties together; it seems like these mountain ranges have a role in keeping all the earth linked.

MARBLE EYE

Amberjack, also known as reef donkeys in certain parts are heavy duty fighters with big broad shoulders matched only by their voracious appetites. Marble eye was the type of fish that could put a bend in your rod, tie a knot in your back, make you hang on to your rod & reel for dear life, causing acute tendonitis in your elbow with every crank, but catching him made you forget all those things, wishing you could do it all over again. One November morning Captain Mike needed to get an early start for the three-hour ride to the ridge of the canyon. Sudden drop offs in water depth, structures of any kind attached like oil rigs, free floating drifting pieces of wood, boxes, or even trees are things to be on the constant lookout for on the open ocean, whether you're looking for fish or not. Mariners always slow down at night as a necessary precaution to avoid running into something. Weeds that form into big long patches that could go on for miles hold a lot of fish, but if you're not careful could clog your engines if you run over them.

Knowing the water temperatures on the surface, all the way down to the thermocline where the temperature changes as you get deeper, keeping an eye out for converging currents, looking out for clear as opposed to murky water, wind direction, moon phases all help in looking for any signs of life on the ocean. Charts, graphs, depth finders, all instruments on your panel are useful tools all good fishermen should know how to use. But there is always a place for old school fishermen's intuition that will never show up on an instrument panel. All good fishermen know to always stay on the lookout constantly. What looks like an empty sea one moment could become the bounty you're looking for the next.

The best and biggest catches often come when you least expect them, keeping the unexpected mysteries of fishing alive, no matter how experienced the fisherman.

The fisherman's task is to stay alert and be ready. Bob's Sr.'s 42 lb snapper & 60 lb gag were prime examples of the unexpected meeting the prepared. Traveling toward another predetermined spot, Captain Mike inadvertently spotted a hump followed by a cliff on his depth finder. "Oh, why not? Let's give it a try here," Captain Mike said. Bob Sr dropped his line a butterflied mullet with a slab of bonito. Bonito are members of the tuna family but they don't share the same meaty qualities. Fisherman joke, if you are going to cook a bonito, it's best to salt it down then let it sit for a while until all the blood is drained out making it ready for cooking. Like all tuna, bonito meat is red when raw then turns white when it's cooked. Placing the blood-drained bonito on a piece of wooden 2x4 on the grill. When the meat turns white, the bonito is ready. You can take it off the grill put it back in your bait box then eat the 2x4…..Bonito meat is tough and too stringy for eating, but they are abundant making great baits for all fish.

Immediately hooking the giant red snapper on his first drop. Nobody really knew how special this snapper would turn out to be. We didn't even know it was a snapper until it reached the surface. Snapper's have a distinct pull, instantly recognizable by the jerking motion you can see on the tip of your rod bobbing up and down. This fish fought more like the 60 lb grouper. Bob Sr. would reel it in soon after. Grouper have a smoother, steadier, usually more explosive pull. The snapper coming up toward the surface looking like a big orange ball of fire resembling the sun. When it did break the surface, its bladder was inflated with air, making it look like a giant beach ball that had just done a belly flop in reverse. A spot found by accident with huge hungry fish on it. The roll of the dice on the unknown spot turned into a pot of luck but we were ready to make it happen…..Back at the dock while still before dawn Captain Mike hollered to all of us who were still bunked in our beds in his finest sailor's language. "GET YOUR ASSES UP!!! We've got some reef donkeys to catch." There is usually a little chill in the air on mid-November mornings. That makes it a touch easier to stay in your bunk just a little bit longer than it usually does in summer. In the salty morning mist, Bob Jr belted out a sneeze HEEEEEEE CHAAAAAA, so loud it could be heard across the harbor over the warming engines of the other boats causing our boat to list on its port side for just a minute as if it might have been hit by a rogue wave in the harbor. "Wait til Bob Jr. reattaches his lungs before boarding," Captain Mike shouted. Everyone laughed. We had set traps in the harbor the night before with the hopes of filling them with choafers and pinfish. The traps can be loaded with anything that might attract fish, in this case we were using shrimp heads we got at a local seafood market. Choafers and pinfish are solid wintertime bait as opposed to the blue runners, herring, cigar minnows, speedo, and the occasional Spanish mackerel that congregate in huge balls by the millions during summertime near the East Pass, our only outlet to the Gulf of Mexico. Catching these baits on a light duty bait rod was sometimes as much fun as going offshore for the "big ones" if you happened to not catch anything as the locals call it getting "skunked," at least you could say you didn't come back empty handed. In the keys they throw nets letting them sink to the bottom then pulling the bait up. Sometimes the nets comes up full, other times empty. It works out OK, but you don't get to feel the pull of all the little bait fish shaking on your line. Sending you an early morning tingle running through your body from head to toe all the way up through your fingers to the tip of the the small rod held in your hand. The bait rod had 10 or 12 little hooks attached to the end of line called a stringer all those baitfish created enough pull to make them a lot of fun to catch especially for kids. "WOW, DID YOU SEE THAT ONE? WOW, THAT'S A BIG ONE. WOW, I CAN'T WAIT UNTIL WE GET A REALLY BIG ONE!!" We always would tell the kids, if you handle the bait gently, they will last longer bringing, you home bigger fish. Make sure when you bait your hook, put the hook through the bait's mouth, not through the eye. Of course when fishing nothing is ever a certainty. For reasons still unknown to anyone on any given day fish will only hit on one type of bait and nothing else, but as Captain Mike would often say when all else failed a fresh live speedo presented to a fish was as tempting as piece of crack to an addict. If that couldn't hook the fish, nothing else could........In addition to live baits we brought along our share of dead baits, usually Boston mackerel and mullett (which were used live or dead) and again a piece of a bonito. The slab scent makes it awfully enticing and difficult for a fish to resist. Sometimes it would even be necessary to combine baits. One thing you could do with a dead Boston mackerel or mullett was use a technique called butterflying. In butterflying, you make an incision along each side of the bait's backbone giving the bait the illusion of having wings when placed underwater. Creating more movement, which meant more bites… All of which factored in on the 42lb. Snapper Bob Sr, brought in, the mullett has on more than one occasion put more than a few groupers in the cooler. Presentation of the bait is as important as the bait itself. If not presented naturally, the fish will turn away from the offering never to be seen again. The Amberjack we were about to encounter made that doubly important. I called him marble eye. Marble eye was an old fish who had been swimming around the depths for years. His skin was wrinkled, and judging from the scratches on his body looked like he had been in a scrape or two probably avoiding the always lurking sharks hanging around the underwater reefs. But OH MAN did marble eye put up a fight. Being blind in one eye made him rely on his other senses more than a younger fish with all his senses intact would have. His blind eye looked like a blue marble and had no pupil. Amberjack can be found anywhere in the water column from bottom to top, unlike groupers or snappers, which are almost exclusively found all the way on the bottom. We dropped another mullet dressed with a slab of bonito and held on. We didn't take the usual 10 cranks off the bottom in hopes of enticing the fish up to give us a head start before he could find a spot on the bottom to hole up in. Once the fish turns his head and finds a spot to hole up in, you can almost always chalk that one up to experience, the fish being the victor. Catching a grouper with 3 or 4 hooks in its mouth from previous battles called jewelry is not uncommon. Finding fish with "jewelry" is possible with the advent of the circle hook, an invention of the modern fisherman. Circle hooks allow the hook to slide to one side of the fish's mouths rather than lodging itself in the middle of the mouth where it could do damage to itself internally if swallowed, also impeding its ability to feed. Old fashioned J hooks that needed removing required a stick about an inch in diameter to be placed down the fishes mouth to where the hook was lodged, sometimes all the way down to the stomach, then spun in a quick circular motion, your line helping create resistance against the hooks setting. Sometimes the fish would get off unharmed. The ones that did not were used as bait or thrown back where a shark or a porpoise could enjoy an easy meal. A circle hook also sets itself in the fish's mouth changing the way bottom fish are caught. There is no need to snatch and jerk when you feel that initial tug. The job of the fisherman becomes to be ready to crank steadily as soon as you get that first strike, not allowing the fish to get his momentum going away from you, otherwise another fisherman will be catching the fish who just adorned himself with your "jewelry." Circle hooks also make it a lot easier for the fisherman to remove the hook from the fish's mouth after bringing him on board. Most bottom-dwelling reef fish have a bladder. The lessening of the water pressure inflates when pulled up through the water column. The bladder must be popped if you want to release the fish, so he can get back down to the bottom. Without popping the air bladder, the fish will stay afloat. All that is needed to pop the bladder is a puncture from a long pointed needle. Sometimes the fish staying afloat can be a saving grace if the fish happens to slip the hook you can easily pull up to retrieve him without the need for a gaff, you can scoop him up the fish falling into your net the way a baseball would fall into a first baseman's mitt on a low throw to first base. Fish with no bladder need to be brought all the way in if they slip the hook the only time you will see them again is in your dreams of what might have been. When battling the pelagic (fish that travel in the open ocean) Captain Mike could always be heard from the bridge saying "In the boat" "In the boat" "In the boat." All you need to take the circle hook out of the fish's mouth is a dehooker, a fancy word for a hook on a stick. Wrap the monofilament once around your hand holding the dehooker in the fish's mouth with your other hand, pulling with an even tension letting the dehooker do the work. A quick short flick of your wrist will make the fish fall off the circle hook straight into your cooler as easily as afternoon droplets fall from the sky in a summer sun shower. Neither fisherman nor fish go through a full season undefeated, unless you are the 1972 Miami Dolphins. You just hope to put more fish on the rack at the end of the day, then there are ones that got away. Sometimes a seemingly small fish can turn out to be the biggest catch of all. Our friend Mike had been on the Twister many times before catching red, white, mingo, mutton, black, and Cubera snapper. But it was the smallest of them, the yellowtail snapper, that make his biggest best most memorable fish story. Mike didn't catch the fish but was an eyewitness to it. Yellowtail are of the smaller variety of snapper but instead of a brush tail their tails are forked V-shaped in what looks like a boomerang. The boomerang action lets them turn their bodies quicker to get away from predators. Bigger yellowtail are called "flags." The one our friend Mike was lucky enough to be on board for definitely qualified as a "flag" he got to see planted.

Ninety eight miles straight west from Naples FL at 2AM in 150 feet of water on an old shipwreck his team landed a 10.8 lb yellowtail snapper good enough for the Florida State record, only less than a pound shy from the world record. Studying the bottom contour of the Gulf of Mexico you can see from Naples. It's a long way out before the continental shelf drops, getting in to the deep water. Mike and his friends ventured out to where few boats dare to go. Their reward was a once-in-a-lifetime fish. The 10.8 lb yellowtail made it all worth it.

Initially marble eye played with the bait. There was a bit of a tug on the line that felt like nibbles, nothing unusual, smaller fish along the bottom like easy meals too. Smaller fish will nibble on your baits until there is nothing left except the hook. Checking your bait the same way you would check your boat's engine filters becomes necessary to keep everything running smoothly.

Bob Sr. cranked his bait all the way up to see if it was still intact then dropped it back down. Slowly cranking he could feel the tension on the line getting tighter. Marble eye, which began by nibbling on the bait, took the mullet and ran, putting a bend in the rod that almost made the tips touch. Captain Mike realized we had a big one then put the throttle in forward. VOOOOOOOM. Bob Sr. again happened to be the lucky one with the rod in his hands. We didn't know what we had on the line. We just knew it was fighting harder than any other bottom fish we had ever encountered. Run after run, marble eye made it clear there was no quit in him. It took some extra fight on our part too to not let marble eye get away. Marble eye made more runs with more tail whipping action than an older fish should have been capable of. An hour later, water bubbles began to be seen on the water surface. All of a sudden a big WOOSH sound accompanied this thing that looked like a giant sea monster breaking through the surface, belly up. Losing his ability to form coherent thoughts, Bob Jr.'s vocabulary had been reduced to repeating the phrase, "HOLY SHIT, HOLY SHIT, HOLY SHIT." It wasn't until getting back to the dock learning the fish weighed in at 110 lbs that he could stop. Running on adrenaline made it impossible to sleep for a week was the prize for bringing marble eye to market.....

Marble eye back at the dock. The adrenaline rush he provided left me unable to sleep for a week. Notice the wrinkle on his lower torso, a sign of his old age.

A FLICKER IN THE WATER

Freshly caught marble eye. That is not a tongue—it is an air bladder that is still full.

BOB GONZALEZ

Lowering marble eye into the cooler.

A FLICKER IN THE WATER

FLICKER IN THE WATER

Part 5

Yellowfin are the most beautiful tuna in the family. Their vibrant colors shine like a rainbow after a ferocious thunderstorm. The elongated yellow dorsal & pectoral fins resembling the curvature of an elongated scimitar sword (an Arabic word) gives them a uniqueness all their own to boast about….." Come a bit closer a little while longer, and you will be ours," we would mutter under our breaths, not wanting to spoil the moment. Two hours and counting since the encounter began, and we were beginning to see the first signs of daylight over the horizon. We didn't know if the fish had any runs left in him, but we still couldn't bring him in too quickly or we could pull the hook out of the fish's mouth. The finesse in which you handle the fight especially when you're getting close to the end is the hallmark of any good fisherman. There is more tension applied on the hook in the fish's mouth the shorter the line becomes. A hasty or rushed movement done in haste could cost you the catch. Steadily and smoothly cranking, we could see the accumulation of line in our reel telling us the fish was now almost within sight. Just a few more cranks then maybe….. this fish had a fighter's spirit taking off again, burning drag. A nice run but we could tell he was tiring, each run becoming shorter than the last. It wouldn't be long now, we said again in hopeful but hushed tones….The big red orange ball in the sky had almost fully made its announcement known. Back in the fight, the fish was now well within range but not yet sighted. Bob Jr. & Gary would be the gaff handlers. One would gaff his mouth, the other his lower torso, hoping to not spoil any meat. 1, 2, 3, 4 cranks when all of a sudden from straight down the silhouette of the fish could be seen for the first time…"Look at the size of that thing," Drawbridge & Captain Mike said from the bridge where they had the most direct view, their hearts beating out of their chests in delirious anticipation. That was brought on partly by lack of sleep by an all night fight with this fish and partly by the disbelief of the size of what they were looking at. Seasoned seaman they were, neither of them had ever seen a yellowfin rivaling this one. Bob Jr. & Gary, each ready with a gaff in hand, approached the back of the boat where the door called a transom is. If the fish could not be lifted, it would have to be brought in through the door by backing the boat down, creating a wave to slide the fish in. Drawbridge came down from the upstairs to give Gary & Bob Jr. an extra Pullman from the rear, in case they might be pulled overboard. Bob Jr. & Gary hunched over the rail and braced themselves, ready to bring in the fish…..Never did we get to weigh that fish, but we all did get to admire it if just for a brief, flickering moment. Its image forged in our minds and seared in our souls forever.

A FLICKER IN THE WATER

The vibrant underwater beauty of the yellowfin tuna, the length of second dorsal fin and the anal fin as well as the finlets between those and its tail distinguish the yellowfin from other tuna's.

First mate Vinni, whose contributions to our team you will read about in subsequent chapters with one of the big yellowfins.

The yellowfins near the tail makes the yellowfins the most beautiful and uniquely designed of all the tuna.

BOB GONZALEZ

The Twister crew: Left to right Bob Jr., Drawbridge, Bob Sr., Captain Mike, with some yellowfins and mahis.

TWISTER IN PARADISE

Twister was a 43 foot Bertram. She had a lengthy career as a top sport fisher before being renamed. Having the battle scars of her previous voyages to prove it. She never went through a customary rechristening process, not wanting to jinx the glory of her past. Sailors in the western hemisphere have always referred to ships in the feminine. Perhaps mariners of ancient times began this tradition because they spent countless hours away from the women in their lives living in a vast, lonely sea. Thinking of their vessel as a she made the long periods of solitude a little easier to cope with. We made a deal with the sea god called Poseidon. Poseidon was the mythical god of the seas, who according to legend kept a log book of every ship he allowed to travel on his oceans. Seafarers who didn't follow his rules would often find bad luck coming to them. Poseidon was the father of Aeolus, the god of wind, who could at a moment's notice be summoned to unleash her wrath on an unprepared vessel. Because of the extraordinary circumstances of Twister's recovery, Poseidon agreed to let us skip the usual rechristening protocols. We wouldn't have to christen her as long as we were kind to her in every other way. Keeping her hull intact, all her instrumentation in working order, her engines clean. And most importantly for us, her refrigerators full. Living solely from your bounty makes for a compelling challenge, hardened sailors of old probably wouldn't have done it any other way, but modern refrigeration is a nice convenience to have. Especially if you happened to get "skunked." Having some sandwiches on board puts everyone in a better mood. Just imagine how many fights on board ships could have been avoided if everyone had a full stomach. Our friend James at the marine store knew exactly how to treat a boat to achieve optimal efficiency. He would always tell us his voice working in coordination with his hands and arms mimicking a scrubbing motion in perfect unison. The most important thing you can do for her hull is "scrub scrub scrub scrub scrub." It will make her happy, keeping her gliding through the waters effortlessly as if propelled by wings. Keeping barnacle growth off her propellers was equally important. It will make her run faster keeping more dollars in your pocket, consuming less of them in the fuel tank. There are some fish in the harbor whose diet included barnacles, namely sheepshead with their tough front teeth, but even they could not completely keep all of it off the propellers. When Twister ran at top efficiency she cruised comfortably between 18 to 20 knots (22 to 23 mph.) Never did James's advice come in more necessary than a time we entered the harbor in Carrabelle, Florida. Carabelle is a beautiful, older small town; its charms remind you of the old American south. Life is slow paced, quiet and peaceful, surrounded by large wooded forests. Bob Jr once saw a black bear near the shoreline in between the trees. When the bear noticed Bob Jr looking at him, he immediately turned running back into the forest. We pulled into the marina late in the afternoon at low tide to refuel having to slow idle through a no-wake zone, taking about two hours to reach the fuel station. The importance disguised the wisdom of what our buddy James had told us about keeping the hull scrubbed became apparent when we crossed over a big rock with only a few inches to spare between the bottom of our hull and the top of the pointed rock. The rock was so close it didn't even register on the transducer to take a reading. If there had been any barnacles attached to our hull we would have scraped the underwater rock, at the very least scratching or denting our hull, or worse ripping a hole in it, which would have meant taking on water. It doesn't get any closer than that without running aground.

As far as Poseidon, we kept our part of the bargain rescuing Twister from the once-in-a-lifetime hurricane called Opal, which had ripped her off her anchor. Opal was an unexpected hurricane that blew up into a sea monster in the Gulf of Mexico overnight. A reminder of nature's mostly beautiful but sometimes ferociously cruel wrath. She was found on her hull parked right in the middle of a busy thoroughfare without any visible signs of damage but needed an airlift to be put back in the water, where she would have to undergo another extensive sea trial. Guaranteeing no bad luck would come to her. Poseidon kept his promise, as did we. Although according to old seaman superstition carrying bananas on board a boat was supposed to bring bad luck. I do remember having done it once. But no bad luck ever came. The closest was a waterspout (a water tornado) that came within a mile before dissipating. Known for being a boat that "raises fish " the sound of her twin 550 horse power engines had raised enough blue marlin to win several local fishing tournaments placing in a few others. In one of the tournaments, we left the dock at midnight instead of the usual sunrise departure, having no choice but to leave in the middle of a lightning storm. If a bolt of lightning hit one of the lightning rods lined straight up one on each side of the boat, the tournament would have been over before it began, frying all the instrumentation. Trying to catch a wink or two before the fishing lines were allowed in the water. Captain Mike went below, leaving Bob Sr. on the helm. The Twister ran a little faster than a lot of the other boats heading out. Bob Sr, concerned he might overrun one of the other slower boats, had to keep watch during the lightning lit sky in between the dark and light of the intermittent lightning strikes to make sure that did not happen. We took her on a maiden voyage to Key West, to fish the annual Hemingway days tournament where we weighed in a prized mahi-mahi. On my next trip I intend to grow back my beard and enter the Ernest Hemingway look-a-like contest. On this trip came our buddy Keith. Keith was a good-natured traveler who loved adventure with a curious mind and who also knew how to get things done. He was what we called a weekly fisherman. Whenever he went fishing, the locals would always tell him he should have been here last week. Or the fish are supposed to be coming through next week. Keith brought along a friend named Paul. Paul had a lot of experience driving tug boats providing us with valuable seamanship information. Keith and Paul made a trip down to Key West with us. The catch of the trip being a 50 lb cobia we saw hanging around an overturned boat, this one fully visible with its hull sticking out of the water. We had some nice catches with Keith. One day on another excursion in the northern Gulf of Mexico, we left the dock from Destin in ideal conditions catching as many groupers and amberjacks as our luck would allow well into the early afternoon when intermittent swells began to develop. First a minute apart then 30 seconds and so on until it came upon us in a fury catching us off guard thrusting us right in the middle of it. The three hour ride back to port was as wild as it was bumpy. KABOOM, a sudden wave hitting the side of the boat would jar us harder than a tackle from a linebacker at the fifty yard line. Nobody got seasick on this trip; everyone was too focused hanging onto a rail trying to stay on their feet. Keith's spirit of adventure in many ways rivaled Drawbridge's. Whereas Drawbridge was single, having more time to indulge his adventures, Keith was married with kids. But that didn't stop him from taking the 23 ft catamaran he had recently purchased for a joy ride across the Gulfstream of the Atlantic ocean. Leaving the dock from Florida in early morning winds of 25 to 30 knots with 12 to 14 foot waves. Keith told his wife, Patty, "Honey, if you don't hear from me by 4PM, call the coastguard." When I spoke to Patty that afternoon, her usual upbeat demeanor was more apprehensive than usual. Luckily he had just enough fuel left in the tank to make it to his destination in the island of Abaco, Bahamas. When he arrived, the dock master was amazed he had even attempted the cross. Saying in his most incredulous tone, "You made it in that?" It was Bob Sr. who once again had the hot hand. Keith had wanted to switch rods, hoping to catch some of that magic for himself. But that was another of those fishing superstitions that were considered taboo. Keith did manage to win that day's catch with a nice Amberjack. Maybe it was the game of risk we played the night before that altered everyone on board except for Bob Sr., who never wanted his hot streak to end in the impending storm. Wanting to venture out even further, Bob Sr., who always liked pushing danger's limits, had once taken a dive into the Destin Harbor when deck chairs that had recently been stitched by hand with the name Twister flew off the boat swept into the harbor in an early evening thunderstorm that could be best described as possessing magnificent all encompassing rage. Bob Jr., content to let the storm pass before retrieving the chairs, could through all the noise of the thunder lightning and unrelenting rain hear from the other side of the dock a loud KERPLUNK. Knowing instantly from a lifetime of experience that Bob Sr. had taken an unwanted dive into the water, there was no other choice but to retrieve him if not the chairs out of the harbor. They could wait. Bob Jr. pulled Bob Sr. from the water and asked, in good humor, "Did you get all wet?" The storm did pass, the chairs were retrieved but never really used again, fishing gear being prioritized. It was not the last time Bob Sr. would find himself in the water unexpectedly. One of the most sacred traditions for the offshore fishermen is the ceremonial dunking in the water back at the dock after catching his first blue marlin. A baptism of sorts. As the boat was pulling out of the dock one morning, Bob Sr. was reaching for one of the ropes he had just untied from the boat's cleat. Aboard the Twister were Bob Sr's. friends Eddie and Joyce from New Jersey. Eddie knows they run out quite a long way to get to the deep water canyons off New Jersey for the yellowfin, making their way up the warm waters of the gulfstream toward Nova Scotia. Today our target was the smaller but no less tasty blackfins, which had been hanging around a part of the Northern Gulf of Mexico called the spur (60 miles due south of Destin) Throwing the rope toward the piling as the boat was pulling out of the dock in hopes of attaching it, Bob Sr. reached out just a bit too far, losing his balance causing him to fall into the water over the side of the boat. The water in the harbor was shallow, only about 10 feet deep. Swimming had been one of Bob Sr.'s passions in his youth. We knew we didn't have to worry about him going under or anything.

The boat had not even made it out from its mooring. Bob Sr. was Ok. He was close enough to shore he swam up to the shoreline rather than being pulled up into the boat, walking out as if had just taken a dip at the beach. As is customary amongst fisherman, we could not resist ribbing him a little bit telling him he looked like Aquaman, coming up out of the water, but in that one instance he started his own blue marlin tradition. All that was required was a change into drier clothes. Eddie and Joyce had the time of their lives. Eddie, who had a porpoise steal one of his baits, had more fun watching the porpoise look up and smile at him coming up close enough to the boat he was able to touch him on the top of his bottlenose than he did catching a fish. Joyce, who had grown up in Mississippi around freshwater lakes, caught her first saltwater fish, a 30 lb blackfin tuna, leaving no doubt Poseidon had blessed the Twister.

A FLICKER IN THE WATER

That is how Twister reappeared after being pulled off her mooring during Hurricane Opal. She was floating on the road which overflowed with water, when the water subsided she was resting comfortably on the pavement. Thankfully she had no interior or exterior damage and continued to provide us with many more thrills for years to come.

Poseidon, the mythical god of the sea. He was a very compassionate god toward his sea travelers as long as you followed his rules of good seamanship. He never went back on his word, and we always treated him and the ocean's with respect.

A FLICKER IN THE WATER

Top photo: Captain Mike, Keith, fresh off of his voyage to the Bahamas
& Bob Sr. Bottom photo working a blue marlin by the side of the boat.
Notice the use of the gloves for handling the line. Fishermen have adapted
since the days Bob Sr. first got his feet wet using only a hand line.

Top photo: Bob Sr., Joyce and Eddie with a mixed rack of grouper, scamp, and blackfin tuna. Bottom photo: Eddie and Joyce with Joyce's first ever saltwater fish, a blackfin tuna. Blackfin tuna are sometimes called footballs because of the size and shape of their bodies. Eddie looks like he wants to carry the tuna in for a touchdown.

APRIL SHOWERS BRING COBIA TOWERS

For northern Gulf of Mexico fishermen, the rite of passage out toward the loop current began in earnest when the skyline on the beach slowly disappeared from view, leaving you with only your compass. It was here where the battle lines between big fish and fisherman were usually drawn. With one notable exception. Cobia season. Cobia, also known as Ling, some call them crab crunchers because of their hard mouth and powerful jaws, brings every other kind of fishing to a halt in spring. They exercise their year-long migration up the Florida coast, coming in closest to shore in the panhandle. It's sight fishing for the persistent. When you spot a cobia you immediately take the boat out of gear, putting the engine in neutral. The boat is driving in the opposite direction of the fish and may need to be turned around in pursuit. Its vital once the fish is spotted not to take an eye off of him, not even for a split second. You may not find him again. Getting close enough to the fish without scaring it away is the key to cobia fishing. You need to get close enough to make as accurate a cast as you can toward the front of the fish. Putting the bait as close to the cobia's mouth as possible, making your bait become irresistible. Eels are their favorites. The eels are kept alive in a bucket of water already hooked so all you have to do is pick up the rod & throw. Eels usually lay in the bucket motionless.

If they were allowed to slither around, they would tangle your line so badly you would have an easier time unraveling the seafaring mysteries of Long John Silver's sunken treasure. Many hours are spent staring at or better yet through the emerald water looking for dark brown spots. Destin is abundantly blessed with sugar white sand on the beaches, providing a background that gives the water its emerald green look. It makes the water clarity better for spotting cobia. Other areas on the coast are not so fortunate. For the patient fisherman, cobia could ordinarily be spotted swimming on the surface riding atop the cresting waves for a leisurely stroll east to west ride toward their spawning grounds. They traveled in large groups called pods, the larger ones tending to travel individually. These pods attracted a lot of attention. Sea turtles, rays, remora, would often be seen hitching their wagons to them for a free safe ride. It was at this time of year when big mako sharks would inevitably find their way closer to the beach, ensuring we were not the only ones in search of cobia. Mako are known for having an extra row of teeth. Their teeth faced opposite to each other for extra shearing. When the water was clear enough and the conditions were right, you could see the cobia a few feet below the surface. We caught our fair share of cobia with the sightseeing technique. Bob Jr. caught a summertime cobia bottom fishing for snapper one year, but that was unusual. That cobia, like many tourists who come to Destin, must have liked it so much he decided to stay permanently. The higher your boat tower, the easier it was to spot them. Twister didn't have a tower; we relied on keen eyesight and sharp accurate casting to catch our cobia. We lost a few too. One was spotted by Bob Jr. at the sea buoy outside the pass. We hooked him, but the drag was too tight, snapping the line. Patty came along for the trip on this day. She enjoyed the outdoors as much as Keith did. Never having seen a cobia caught before, we handed her the rod hoping to get her, her first cobia. She got to see the fish swallow the bait whole, a thrill in itself before the line snapped. Patty was a good sport about it. She took pleasure in all the porpoise seen swimming around the boat. It's hard to resist, but it's better not to hand feed or throw food to the dolphins. It makes them dependent on handouts, unable to fend for themselves in their natural element. At certain times of the year, depending on water temperature, prehistoric fish known as tripletail could be seen. A fish with three tails that looked like a baseball umpire's brush, tripletail have been traversing the seas since mankind began fishing with the rudimentary use of nets & harpoons. They are not the prettiest looking fish in the ocean, having flaky rough skin and a funny looking short round body, but they are among the tastiest. Very selective feeders, they are worth the extra time it takes to coax them to take your bait. Porpoise are so friendly we would see them everywhere from right on the beach to 100 miles offshore. Inshore they would often follow a fish hooked on your line usually a king mackerel called silver kings. They would play with them with their noses but rarely did they steal them from you. Seeing them offshore gave us a feeling of friendly companionship on what otherwise at times could be a dark, desolate ocean. Having a lot of porpoise around meant the area was in all likelihood not inhabited by sharks, porpoise being their natural enemies. On another trip, a cobia of monster size had come right up at the bait we threw at him. He had a gleam in his eye salivating at the temptation of our offer on his lips touching the bait before at the last moment turning away. Had our friend who was with us presented the bait properly, that fish story would have had a better ending. He let the bait sink instead of giving the bait vibrancy, making it look alive by jiggling it. Oh well, there's always the next one. Going down swinging is as much part of the game of baseball as losing a fish is, we would always say, but it's a lonelier ride back to the dock after losing a nice fish, just like it is walking back to the dugout right after a strikeout. In between these periods of frantic excitement, there were long stretches of tedium, which could lead to dozing off. You can only stare at the water for so long before your eyes began to glaze over. Anytime Captain Mike noticed someone nodding off, he would blow the boat horn loudly into your ear. The sound would wake you and shake you. The frequency was so unpleasant it kept you up for hours. After a few repeated instances of this happening, not wanting to repeat the experience, Bob Jr. decided to take matters into his own hands. Better yet by his own fingertips. That evening back at the dock, when all was quiet for the day, Bob Jr. flipped the breaker off for the horn in the breaker box.

He knew the breaker horn was usually taken for granted and overlooked. Knowing they would be going out again the following day, he wasn't going to have that horn again bellowing in his ear. True to form another long day of sighting cobia required the use of the horn. When Captain Mike reached for the switch, nothing happened except the "sound of silence." Not wanting to tell anyone just yet the problem was the turned off breaker, Bob Jr. let Captain Mike stew for the rest of the day wondering what was wrong with the horn. Was it an electrical problem? Was there something else wrong also? Is there anything I have been doing that caused this malfunction? The next day was scheduled as an off day & Capt. Mike would be working on the boat all day. He spent three hours in the blazing midday son researching the boat from the engine room inside the hull to where all the electrical components were housed up on the bridge. Stumped, Capt. Mike retired to his home for the evening. It was then Bob Jr. decided to pull the plug on his prank. He called Capt. Mike telling him, "Gee Mike, I finally figured out what the problem is with the horn."

"Oh really, what?" Capt. Mike said excitedly. "I turned the breaker off," Bob Jr. said, trying to contain his laughter. On the other end of the line complete silence that lasted only for a few seconds but seemed to last for hours was the only thing that could be heard. The horn episode was never repeated. Our focus now would turn offshore....

A FLICKER IN THE WATER

Eddie on the left and Bob Sr. with a spring cobia.

Bob Jr. with another springtime cobia.

A FLICKER IN THE WATER

The prehistoric tripletail. They look like they have three tails but actually they only have one, the typical tail in the middle, the other two are fins. During cobia season sometimes they are seen close to the beach on the water surface. Other times they are seen way offshore, usually hanging around or underneath sargassum seaweed. Don't let their odd looks fool you—they are a very tasty, good-eating fish.

BOB GONZALEZ

Cobia, they are not the prettiest looking fish in the sea, but they are one of the tastiest.

SHRIMP GUMBO FISH JUMBO

The shrimp boat we approached that we immediately knew would pay dividends later aligning ourselves with felt like a pairing of nuptials at sea. She looked innocent enough, resting calmly in what today was a sea of tranquility during the day with her trawl nets raised. All aboard were resting after a hard night's haul. Overnight trips were always the most unpredictable as well as the most productive. The ice cooler, the fuel, and the moods of weather were the instruments that gauged your trip. As long as they held up, so could we. Blackfin tuna, the smallest of the tuna in the family shaped like footballs, were all around. Many times wary of any oncoming vessel they recognized as an intruder, this time they didn't seem to notice us, and if they did they didn't seem to care. All around as far as the eyes through our binoculars could see, huge schools of blackfins were "busting" (feeding) on the water's surface. The noise they made as they leapt from one small meal to another, their tails flapping in the air then slapping the water as they came back down was deafening. Mimicking the sound of tossed hand grenades, looking like a field laid of land mines exploding everywhere. Enough shrimp had fallen through the previous night's shrimp nets to attract not only blackfin tuna but every other species of fish inhabiting the Gulf of Mexico. There were no oil rigs or structures of any kind. Just open ocean where one shrimp boat would create for us one of the best catches we ever had. Heading straight south from Destin, we stopped to bottom fish on the way out, wanting to put some fish on the boat as a sign at least in our minds of good things to come before starting our next day's pelagic troll. The sea floor was too deep to drop a chain anchor. Overnight trips would require the use of a sea parachute to keep the boat's bow straight into the oncoming wave of the current. This is especially important if the seas happen to be choppy. A boat taking on the wave straight on was easier to handle for those of us onboard making it much safer than taking waves off the boats side. Boats not deploying a parachute could easily find themselves 15 or 20 miles away from their original location at sunrise being dragged by the currents. Whereby a boat with a parachute would only be a mile off its location. A sea anchor had to be put out properly to achieve its desired result. If not deployed properly, it could become a hazard. Heavy duty rope was fastened in a bow knot to a cleat on the windward side of the boat then carefully dropped into the water. Closer to the parachute itself, there were many smaller threads of thick string that needed to be kept free of entanglement so the parachute would open properly, filling with water. On this occasion, our friend Drawbridge put out the parachute too soon before making sure the threads were properly separated. Instead of opening up and clearing away from the boat into the current, the parachute headed straight back toward the stern becoming entangled in the propellers. Drawbridge, always the adventurer, volunteered to jump in the water to cut the parachute's strings. Jumping into the ocean 60 miles from shore in 6,000 ft. of water at dusk with a lot of sharks lurking underneath was something only a free spirit like Drawbridge would relish doing. The only thing Drawbridge had in his favor was the water temperature was around 80 degrees in summer and he would not be down in the water, very long so he didn't need to put on a wetsuit to protect himself from the possibility of hypothermia. A set of flippers would do. We thought about tying a rope around his waist in case he got caught up in the current but decided to keep the dinghy we had on our bow on standby instead. The dinghy was a nice little raft made out of hard rubber with a fiberglass bottom. She carried with her a 10 horsepower engine that had come in handy whenever smaller tasks were required. Ten horsepower on a rubber raft could lift you off the water as if you were riding an elevator shaft. We used the dinghy many times to cross the harbor. Having only one small engine, we always hoped it would not stall at the wrong time. Taking his sharpest knife and best pair of goggles, Drawbridge jumped in the water, cut the strings from the propellers, and we retrieved the parachute that was still attached to the boat's cleats. We pulled Drawbride back on board with one of the gaffs we used as a rod pulling him up then sliding him in through the transom door. Drawbridge and we were the luckiest people on the Gulf that early evening. A mere 5 minutes after getting Drawbridge back on the boat, a 15 foot hammerhead swam right underneath us so close you could see eyeballs scouring through the water on each side of his giant hammerhead. The hammerhead had arrived just a few minutes late to the party, trailing Drawbridge's fresh scent. For years to come I would kid Drawbridge telling him that hammerhead wasn't after him. He just wanted a free beer. Fishing continued on well into the evening. We caught several medium sized (80 lb) yellowfin tuna right as the sun set, giving us a symbolic taste of what would hopefully be a good catch the following day.

    The next day's fishing went better than we ever expected. The fish following the smorgasbord buffet left behind by the shrimp boat were fired up in a frenzy of action. At high noon, Bob Sr. got a tremendous pull on the line while seated in the fighting chair. The fighting chair helps give the fisherman leverage against a big fish. Bob Sr. lifted his rod off the chair, placing it in one of the rod holders on the side of the boat to position himself for the fight. Bob Jr. who was guiding the chair by having it pointed toward the line was so focused on the line he kept hold of the chair, guiding it even after Bob Sr. had gotten up. A two hour give & take in the now 90 degree day ensued. Excited by what we thought was a giant tuna, we didn't pay much attention to the other fish around us. Coming toward us, Bob Sr looked over the stern turned around yelled in a strong, somewhat surprised, somewhat disappointed voice. "IT'S A SHARK." We had just fought one of the biggest bull sharks you will ever see. I'm sure if we had taken this shark in to be weighed it would have challenged some longstanding records. And the shark was angry. REAL ANGRY. Bull sharks are very aggressive; it doesn't take much to rile one up, this one being no exception. Sharks are nature's ultimate predators, equipped with seemingly supernatural survival mechanisms. Great Whites are a wonder of the natural world. Only the divine hand of a grand designer could have created such a marvelous creature, having survived on the world's oceans for millions of years. Great Whites are capable of detecting one drop of blood in 10,000 gallons of water. The one thing they are not capable of is being held in captivity—man has yet to figure out how to do that. I like to think of it as a reminder that both man & creature are meant to be free, surviving in God's open spaces. Hammerhead with their flat hammers can identify electrical impulses as low as a 10 watt bulb from fish buried beneath the sandy bottom from miles away. All of them can grow new sets of teeth as they need them. Their bodies are filled with cartilage, not bones that become brittle over time like most other fish. They can survive out of water for days at a time. A reminder if you ever bring one back to the dock to never take their being dead for granted, no matter how they might appear. Bull sharks can adapt to freshwater, something they alone among the sharks are uniquely blessed with the adaptability to do, being spotted miles inland up rivers and estuaries. Perhaps their most unique quality is the way they urinate. Instead of secretion through their gills or in most cases an organ, unlike most sea life they urinate by absorbing excess fluid in their body cavities excreting the excess through their skin. We cut the line by the side of his mouth, letting him go. Then turned our attention onto the other fish.

Shrimp boats usually have a lot of fish nearby feeding off of the scraps that fall through their nets.

BOB GONZALEZ

Around the shrimp boats or out in the open ocean you can see a lot of flying fish. They propel themselves from the water evading predators, their bodies and wings working symmetrically to glide through the air anywhere from just above the surface to twenty feet above the water covering usual distances of 160 ft., but can catch the updrafts created from the waves to glide up to 1,300 feet.

A FLICKER IN THE WATER

Bob Sr. and Bob Jr. with competing red snappers.

DRAW YOUR SWORD

Bottom fish stay in one general area all year round, moving to different bottom spots whether they be shipwrecks, artificial reefs, or natural bottoms. Colder water temperatures bring them closer to shore in winter. During spawning season, they would sometimes float on the water surface. Their feeding behavior is more predictable and more reliable than their traveling cousins, who could be found on most days more eager to devour one of your offerings. Though not always. Not long after the attacks on the World Trade Center in September of 2001, our buddies Steve and Vinny came out for a bottom fishing trip with us. In addition to the usual snapper and grouper we would also target triggerfish. There are many species of triggerfish, most having bright brilliant colors. They all have a hard bone coming out of the upper part of their spine that looks like a trigger with a 2nd trigger like bone on the lower part of their spine that acts like a release mechanism. Triggerfish may be the most romantic fish in all the sea. They are very territorial in protecting their nesting areas, having been known to bite divers who venture into their territory. Male triggerfish are known to mate with up to ten different females in the same day during the mating season. Steve was a local captain who chartered his own boat. For him not having to take on the captain's normal duties for a day at sea was a welcome relief. Vinny had a reputation as being a high-energy guy who lived to fish and was often Steve's first mate. "I'm ready to go, Skip," Vinny would often be heard saying before the other mate's had even made it down to the dock. Vinny could go full steam ahead, sunrise to sunset. After a long day on the return trip, it was Vinny who was usually putting all the gear away, making sure all the hooks were tied to the rod properly and also making sure all the leads were tightly fastened around the reels, so they could not swing around hitting anyone. Vinny was an expert with a filet knife in his hand as we all were. One of the most gratifying pleasures for fishermen is the looks of curious anticipation on the people's faces standing at the dock as you're backing your boat in on the day's return. After backing in, tying the boat to its pilings, the crowd is eager to see what the day brought and stands at attention as the top of the cooler gets lifted. The dock gets sprayed down with freshwater then the fish one by one get thrown on the dock. "Oh wow, look at that one. Oh man, what kind is that?" they ask from the crowd. If there happens to be a really big or unusual catch on board, we try to get them at peak excitement then bring that one out last. The fish get hung on a rack and then any of us but usually Vinny his natural enthusiasm entertaining the crowd while he filets the fish with stories of how they were caught. Giving the process an authenticity, he sharpens his knife on an old fashioned sharpening stone as the onlookers ask, " What bait did you use? Oh man, how deep was the water? Was it rough out there?" Vinny always made sure to strip the filets just right. Cutting out the bloodline, the darker colored line that looks like a stripe running along the fish's torso, was always priority number one. Taking out the bloodline keeps the flavor of the fish meat intact. Then he made sure to take out all the bones. For the real conservationists, there's saving the nutritious fish head which is loaded with vitamins and minerals makes a great fish soup. Never running out of stories to tell, Vinny could keep them entertained for hours. After the September 11th attacks, everyone was on edge, not knowing if the attacks would be limited to airplanes in New York City. Living on the coastline close to two Air Force bases, we were not sure if they would be considered a target. Modern day pirates still sail around the world's oceans. Every once in a while we would hear stories of vessels that had been raided, never to be heard from again. We thought it might be an opportune time for piracy to increase. Ready for whatever might happen, we made jokes to ourselves if pirates ever attempted to raid us we could scare them off with our looks alone. We even made up our own pirate song, sung it a capella with our fishing rods used as air instruments, called, "Seafaring Pirates of OLD." Seafaring Pirates of OLD: Only cared for sea treasures truth be TOLD: In seas indescribable rough hot windy or COLD: The continuous search for blubbered mammal never quenched their lusty thirst for GOLD: Nothing not even the oceans breezy crosswinded SWIRL: High atop the ship lookout post could stop the search for the oceans jeweled PEARL: Skull & Bones flag UNCURLED: Flying high atop the ship mast UNFURLED: Getting in our sworded swashbuckling WAY: Was never a good idea, you were always made to PAY: A finished job was never final your reward for coming back empty with trailed smelly SKUNK: Was a round barrel of old pirate ale whiskey making a peg-legged pirate slippery DRUNK: Before taking the long walk down the short PLANK: Skunked pirate on board until the boat of its own weight SANK.

Steve was half Indian with a dark olive complexion with a long, thick beard that could make any pirate fancying himself as Captain Kidd shiver in his boots. Bob Sr. & Bob Jr. were both Latin. Bob Jr. also carried a beard at the time he along with Steve both wore bandanas for added effect. Taking on this appearance did bring on certain disadvantages. One day while we were just cruising outside the harbor letting the boat's engines run, a marine patrol became curious as to what we were doing. For an hour he followed our every move, trailing us all the way back to the marina until we tied up at the dock. He got out of his patrol boat walking calmly but suspiciously toward us. After some small talk he asked us to open our cooler. Only the patrol man knows what he was suspicious of. We opened the cooler. The cooler was empty just having some flotation devices inside. He turned around and told us good luck before leaving, never bothering us again. After that encounter, Bob Jr. shaved his beard, but he kept wearing his bandana. The bottom fish must have been a little nervous as well because we didn't even get a single bite that day. We would have to wait for nightfall. During the day between swells, Bob Jr. spotted a whale shark perpendicular to the water. Usually you will see a fish horizontal in the water but it was unusual seeing one with the tail pointed down toward the ocean floor with his head up to the water line. It looked like a vulnerable position for a fish to be in, making him susceptible to attack. Whale sharks are the biggest of all the shark species by far. So big that normally aggressive predators may have been scared to attack. But they are as gentle as a light sea breeze. Brave souls have gone in the water to swim around with them, hitching a ride on their dorsal fin on top of their back. Something that Drawbridge would not even do. This one was opening and closing his gills engulfing all the plankton he could pile into his gills, which they use as a filter, in one big gasp. It made a sound similar to a whale when he breaches the surface to open his blowhole. "WOOSH" Daytime had not produced much, but nighttime would become a different story. Most of the night we spent watching sea turtles, baitfish, flying fish, whatever was drawn to the lights from the boat's bridge. All of that stopped suddenly when the mysterious denizen of the deep, the mighty swordfish, would come calling. Contemporary fishermen are using daytime techniques to catch swordfish. In our time we fished for them strictly during the night. Attaching a glow stick about the size of a cigar to the line. Swordfish have huge eyeballs about the size of a billiard ball, giving them the ability to absorb a lot more light than most fish. They also are one of the few fish that produces their own body heat, allowing them to stay deep for long periods of time without having to resurface. On occasion fishermen do see them lying on the water's surface absorbing the sun's heat rays during daylight, regenerating their lost energy. Glow sticks were dropped one hundred to 300 feet down with the hope of drawing a swordfish up attracted by the light. On the hook would be their favorite live bait, squid. In case the squid did not get any bites, we had some octopus as a backup option. Be careful not to agitate the squid, and always keep them away from your eyes. We needed to remind ourselves. Squid and octopus have some similarities. Both will shoot ink in an act of self defense at their attackers, both have the ability to camouflage into their surroundings, and both are highly intelligent & unlike most creatures in the sea rely on sharp superior eyesight to stay safe from predators. Their differences are even more pronounced. Instead of the customary one heart that most sea life has, octopuses have three hearts: two hearts pump blood to their gills, the other heart pumps blood to the rest of the body. While squid and octopus both have multiple arms the squid uses one brain to send information to all its limbs. Octopuses use nine brains; each arm has its own brain that works independently. How they transfer that information so quickly is anyone's guess, but the swordfish love them. After the long, unproductive daylight hours, Bob Jr. asked everyone. "Can we borrow at least one of those octopus brains for tonight? The fish are outsmarting us at the moment." The plan worked when out of the midnight blue a late night swordfish took the bait and ran. *Zzzzzz Zzzzz* whoop whoop went the line. The fight in the dark was on. Captain's insomnia was the correct way to describe Captain Mike's affliction. Once the engines got revved at the dock he left his sleep at home. Fish have the innate ability to keep men awake. Or maybe the other way around. Whatever the cause, Captain Mike was on the line when the fish struck. Bob Sr. would be charged with the gaff, Bob Jr., the transom door. It was pitch dark with hardly any stars or moon in the night sky giving the water little to no reflection to see what was happening on the water surface. This fight was fought strictly by touch, hearing, and feel necessitating all of our fishermen's instincts. After a few runs the swordfish came up close to the boat. First we heard the splash, then we saw the body. Bob Sr. gaffed the fish through the dorsal fin, missing his body entirely. The swordfish in a fit of rage pounded the water around the boat. Bob Jr., instead of flipping the transom door in an upward counterclockwise motion. tried to push it forward, nearly tearing it off its hinges. Realizing what he was doing, he opened the door, letting the fish come in. With one swing of the tail, the fish made his presence known when he hit the floor deck. Shaking the floor like a bag of concrete had been dropped from the top of the bridge shaking everyone to their core generating a sound like a loud thud. The swordfish body was thicker, more powerful, and broader than any fish we had ever caught before. The tail end of the body was almost as rounded as the upper torso. His broadbill was longer, flatter, and seemingly built stronger than other billfishes, the flatter shape made like it was used for shearing. Other billfish, like marlin and sailfish, have sharp, round, pointed bills in the shape of a spear made for stabbing. After being subdued, the swordfish was kept on ice, covered in a blanket, then brought back. He weighed in at 450 lbs.

Late-night, early-morning swordfish. It felt like a ton of bricks had fallen on the deck when he pounded on it with his tail.

Bob Sr. working a bottom fish. Nice bend on the rod, as soon as you drop that bait you have to be ready for the bite.

A FLICKER IN THE WATER

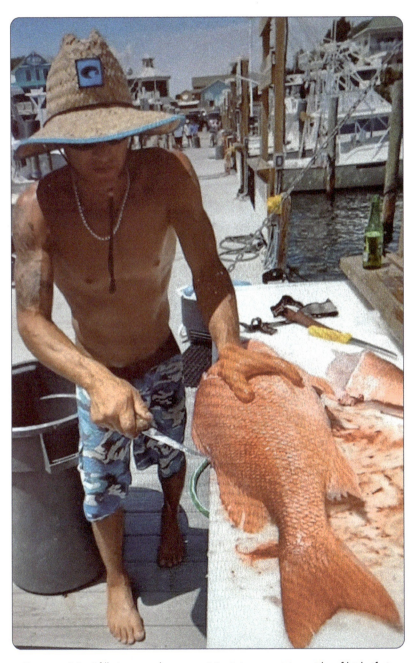

First mate Vinni filleting a red snapper. Vinni, is a magician with a filet knife in his hands. He is as good of an entertainer at the dock as he is a fishermen.

Captain Steve on the left, with Bob Sr., Bob Jr., first mate Vinni, & crew. That is a rare summertime cobia in the middle, usually a springtime fish. There are some that stay all year round.

A FLICKER IN THE WATER

There are approximately forty different species of triggerfish, some of them with incredible color combinations such as the titan, the clown, the Picasso, and the queen triggerfish, most of which make the Pacific ocean their habitat. The one pictured here is a gray triggerfish, the species most common to the Gulf of Mexico. They are notoriously ill-tempered and protect their territory ferociously when intruded (even by scuba divers). Besides being a good food fish, the other thing triggerfish share in common are the two dorsal fins that look like triggers which when agitated serve as a defense mechanism. The larger trigger can only be unlocked by depressing the smaller secondary trigger.

CALL IT A FLUKE

Hardy fishermen at sea crave freshwater like a parched tree in a dry desert. But this water is no mirage. Soda, juices, are best left at home. Water is the great thirst quencher. You could feel the water hydrating the cells in your body, cooling and soothing your insides from the first sip until the last gulp. Water plainly lacking in taste on land miraculously becomes very tasty navigating its way through a sunny, sea-salted pallet, unless that is you happen to develop a queasy stomach. Then the drink of choice becomes manmade good old-fashioned ice-cold beer. Sailors of old have been using this well kept secret to counter the effects of seasickness for centuries. Pirates of old drank rum, and merchant sailors drank beer. YO HO HO and a bottle of rum. Get out of the way to get me some! Bob Sr. as a young fisherman in New Jersey had gone out fishing on a long holiday weekend when he would have to put that old sea hymn to the test. His and 19 other boats left the dock early before sunrise, targeting fluke. Flukes are a flat bodied fish living almost exclusively on the seafloor. Upon untying the ropes from its pilings and setting out from the dock, Bob Sr. knew it was going to be a long, rough day. Without having had beer on hand, he may have suffered the same fate as most of the other fishermen who spent most of the day below deck, making love to an ordinary bait bucket, turning it into a fish-inducing chum bucket, missing out on the good sea fortune that awaited him. Having worked the bottom tirelessly the whole day without any luck when on the very last drop he felt the tug he was waiting for. These are the moments that bring the seasick back to life. Proving once again anything can happen when a fishing line is put in the water with the right preparation. Pulling up a 9.3 lb fluke with little time to spare. Bob Sr. had a real good chance of winning the first-place prize out of all twenty boats tough enough to go out bravely facing the elements that day. Caught so late In the day, Bob Sr.'s boat needed to be back to the dock by 6 o'clock to make the day's official weigh in. The captain said on the way in he had not seen a fluke that size for several years, thinking it had a real good chance of winning the day's prize. He also wanted to make it back on time. Captains, like everyone, are very competitive with reputations to build and uphold. Any big fish brought in on their boat is a source of prideful bragging rights for years to come. Pulling into the dock with 10 minutes to spare they were the 18th boat back to weigh in fish, leaving only 10 minutes and two boats left to go. As expected Bob's Sr. fluke had taken the lead with the next closest fish weighing in at 5.1 lbs. No way his big fluke could be overtaken, he thought. Or could it? There was a lot of commotion on the final two boats as they approached the dock as if they had plans to spoil Bob Sr.'s last second fluke with a giant fluke of their own. They showed off the huge fluke, triumphantly holding it up in the air for all to see while backing into the weigh station. Groans of Oohh's and Ahh's could be heard rumbling up and down the dock. The crowd stunned into silence as the fish was hoisted on the scale. 10.2. The bright yellow light meter on the scale flickered on and off as the fish swayed back and forth in the early evening sea breeze, now blowing at a steady 30 knots. Bob Sr.'s hopes shattered by this unexpected turn of events. The seasickness he was suffering from earlier quickly turned to land sickness, feeling sucker punched in the pit of his stomach. After a lengthy consultation with the captain, allowing drama to build, the officials about to reward the day's purse to the 10.2 lb. fluke turned to the crowd and said, "Pay no attention to the fish on the scales. He is disqualified."

"How could this be?" the people in the crowd wondered aloud. The fish is made out of rubber, therefore not a real fish. April Fools' Day. Many in the crowd who were in on the prank laughed as the announcement was made. Unbeknownst to Bob Sr., it was an April Fools' Day tradition practiced every year. Relieved and feeling better again, Bob Sr. took to the podium accepting the day's winning 1st place prize of $500. Having recently arrived in the U.S. from Cuba, Bob Sr. said afterward feeling that stack of $1 bills in his hand felt like he had just won the lottery. Call it a fisherman's tale. Or…

Call it a fluke!

Fluke, also known as summertime flounder, is a flat-bodied fish that lays on one side on the sandy bottom. The top side is dark and has two eyes, the bottom side is completely white.

A FLICKER IN THE WATER

Not a fluke, Bob Jr. as a teen fisherman with a couple of New Jersey bluefish.

INTRACOASTAL LIVING

Thank goodness for intracoastal waterways, nature's as well as sometimes man made safer havens of alternative shipping routes. Used mainly for trade, moving cargo as well as shortening distances of sea travel or just good old fashioned recreation, intracoastal waterways play a large role for mariners. Saving them mostly a lot of money, time, sometimes even saving their life. As we were about to learn for ourselves. On the return trip from Key West with Bob Sr. assuming captain's duties, the seas got so rough they became impassable. After a few years we became experienced at anticipating the weather patterns knowing when & how strong the fronts pushing through would be, using marine forecasts as a guide. But in this instance we were still at the mercy of the storms whims having not yet acquired the knowledge necessary to make a good determination. Were it not for the waterways we would have been stuck in an unfamiliar port with little to no provisions until the storm passed. Waterways made hopping up Florida's west coast around the big bend to the panhandle safe, easy, and fun. We made our way to Apalachicola. Apalachicola was once known for its world famous oysters, producing 90% of Florida's oysters. Today it is home mainly to shrimpers and coastal fishermen. Oysters do remain and we saw a sheepshead crush an oyster shell with its front teeth. Sheepshead are small fish with a human looking row of front teeth, but they are much tougher than human teeth. If humans tried to crush an oyster shell with their front teeth, they would need to pay a visit to their dentist. From Apalachicola to Destin we navigated the inland bays and rivers. It was a relief of sorts traveling these often-overlooked beautiful backways. The scenery is magnificent as Bob Jr says. We finally arrived back in Destin out of harm's way, ready to fish. On these intracoastal waterways the funniest thing to happen to us could almost qualify as a zany cartoon caper. Drawbridge, now fully back in the captain's chair, looked for more adventure after returning from the tournament in Cabo San Lucas. His escapade upon arriving in Mexico with a boat full of Sol beer had gotten him detained, carrying a small fine. He was happy being back at the helm, driving his boat across Florida on the Lake Okeechobee waterway. The waterway where the Gulf of Mexico connects with the Atlantic ocean. Out of the corner of his eye through an unusually thick early morning fog that had developed on the lake Drawbridge noticed what at first he thought was your typical Florida alligator or possibly even a crocodile in the lake. Crocodiles are bigger than alligators and could adapt to salt and freshwater. Alligators strictly inhabit freshwater. In a scene you would think came from a cartoon, Drawbridge then saw a man wearing suspenders jump in the water behind what he thought was an alligator. Puzzled, Drawbridge dismissed it, thinking maybe it was just a man playing with his dog. Lake Okeechobee is wide and long but not very deep, averaging just 11 feet in depth with many no-wake zones to navigate through. Drawbridge noticed that they were not slowing down and suddenly heard a strange sound in the distance like a grunt, still not able to determine what it was. Due to the fog cover thickness it was impossible to see anything Drawbridge had to rely solely on his ears. Driving through thick fog in Florida on a lake can make it seem like you're driving through a glass of milk. He approached where the sound was coming from slowly when the man in the water belted out, "It's not an alligator…it's my pig. The pig got away from me as I was trying to move him." Pigs are often very aggressive and those potbellied ones with those horns on their nostrils can do a lot of damage to you and your equipment if you are not careful. Not wanting to harm the pig, Bob Jr. who was with Drawbridge threw a bait net over the pig, corralling him until the farmer came over shortly after. We pulled the farmer safely on board when he then helped bring the pig up into the boat. Drawbridge drove the boat to the shoreline and dropped off the farmer again, reunited with his pig. The farmer thanked him, saying on the way back he would be willing to trade his 250 pound pork pig for 250 pounds of fish.

BOB GONZALEZ

Drawbridge back and ready for more adventure. A little shark blood never bothered him. We threw this one back.

A FLICKER IN THE WATER

Bob Sr. & Jose with a Gag grouper.

PROPELLERS IN THE MIST

Early morning mist did not prepare us for the unforeseen bite of a different kind we would experience later in the afternoon. The day again started before sunrise. Another of our buddies known as Keychain Dan told us about the wahoos that were hanging out about forty miles offshore underneath some floating debris. The nickname Keychain arose when the lock on a boat Dan owned many years before was stuck unable to power its outboard engines off, necessitating a locksmith to come unlock them. But not before burning out all the fuel in the tank, requiring a sea tow to come back into port. Ever since before every trip it became customary to ask, "Hey Dan, did you bring your lucky keychain?? Hey Dan, did you bring that extra fuel we might need?? Hey Dan, do you remember the number for Sea Tow??" A party of five left the dock looking for the wahoo. Sure enough when we got there at 7AM on the very first drop we got a strike before the bait even made its way to the bottom. That was just the first one, for the next three hours the bite sizzled hot. So hot Bob Jr. on a mid-depth two hooked lure brought in a wahoo on the back hook and a mahi on the front at the same time. Bringing in a dozen more wahoos of the snake variety. (I'll explain where the snake term comes from in the next chapter) on board. Snakes usually hang together in schools, while bigger wahoos tend to swim alone, but the meat is super tasty. Besides, being the fastest swimmers in the ocean, wahoo might be the best-tasting saltwater fish of all. Similar to most pelagic fish when hooked their bodies become aglow, (become lit) is the common term. Electricity emanates from them as bright as a plugged in fully lit Christmas tree decorated with tinsel. When fishing for wahoo or king mackerel the most important part of the preparation is having plenty of wire leaders ready before heading out from the dock. Wire leaders put at the end of the line leading all the way up to the hook will save the fisherman a lot of lost fish. Wahoo and king mackerel teeth will cut through a monofilament line like a sharp filet knife does, filleting a fish back at the dock. We spent a few more hours landing schooling mahi, one of them about 20 lbs, before making our way back toward the dock. Arriving back just a few miles offshore from the beach with a couple of hours of sunlight remaining we threw a line in the water looking to catch some king mackerel. To the untrained eye it might be easy to mistake a king mackerel for a wahoo. Their body shapes are similar. Looking closely at a king mackerel you can see a long black stripe running down the body cavity the wahoo does not have. Their fight when hooked is also very similar. Kings like wahoo will take a bait running away from you, then do a quick unexpected about face swimming right back toward you. To the inexperienced fisherman it feels like you lost the fish, but it's at this point in the fight when it becomes critical to crank as fast and as hard as you can to keep tension in the line. If the fisherman allows the line to get any slack in it the hook could easily slip out of the fish's mouth. King mackerel normally are found closer to shore in murkier water than their close cousins. Wahoos like clearer, deeper water in the open ocean space where they use their extraordinary speed to find their prey. Using their speed, the wahoo will overrun their quarry then wait for it to come in front before striking. Marlin, mahi, sailfish and others like to chase from behind. It's an unforgettable thrill to see a trailing fish catch up to your bait then retreat again, catching up until finally exploding on your bait. Bob Jr. was the lucky one trolling a cigar minnow along the beach when a thirty five pound king mackerel swallowed his bait whole in one gulp. It didn't take long to get this king to the boat. Pulling it in with the gaff, we didn't know why the king was swimming toward the boat faster than they normally would, almost wanting to jump into the boat. We got the answer when a big bull shark probably attracted by all the commotion in the splash came up biting one of the propellers. The wash from the spinning propellers probably made the shark think there was a lot of baitfish to be had. The bull shark, relentless in its pursuit, kept lunging at the slowly turning propellers moving the boat forward at about 10 knots, going down then coming back up again. We tried speeding up then slowing down almost to an idle trying to discourage the shark, but no matter what we tried we just couldn't shake him. This bull shark had his mind made up—he wanted to eat and nothing was going to stop him. The bull had disfigured one of the propellers when it was idle while we gaffed the king mackerel. If the propellers had been in motion, even the thick-skinned bull would have been shredded to pieces. Boat propellers are made from bronze, making them resistant to the elements. The shark bent the propeller so easily, making it look like it was made of cardboard. On its last lunge, the bull got closer to the inside of the boat than any of us would have liked. He took a lunge forward coming up out of the water, hitting his head on one of the outboard engines trying to take a bite. A tooth came flying out of its mouth landing on the stern at Bob Sr.'s feet. That was the last we saw of that bull shark. We're sure he went away unharmed though—the shark could grow a new tooth back in a week. The boat was not as fortunate. We limped back into the marina on one propeller instead of two. The damaged propeller needed to be replaced, as did some of the fuel lines running to the engine. At least we had a cooler full of fish to enjoy. Getting "skunked" after that would have been tougher to swallow for us than the boat's propeller.

BOB GONZALEZ

Bob Sr. and Bob Jr. with a wahoo and mahi that bit on the same two hooked lure at the same time.

A FLICKER IN THE WATER

Mingo snapper, they make great bait as well as a great fish to eat.

BOB GONZALEZ

Bait fishing at sunrise. Bait fish congregate by the millions in Destin mainly because of its water clarity.

SAN SALVADOR (THE NEW WORLD)

Driving over the Destin bridge for the first time out overlooking the Gulf of Mexico, on what was once called Florida's forgotten coast, Bob Jr. never had any inkling he would one day be fishing the emerald green waters he was admiringly surveying, being drawn in by the natural beauty surrounding him. The only thought entering Bob Jr.'s mind was the overwhelming feeling as if he was making some sort of a modern day New World discovery. "WOW!" he said to himself, caught in a time warp. This is what Christopher Colombus must have felt like when after many months at sea he stumbled upon land on his first voyage to what he believed was a new world in October of 1492. Navigating at the mercy of where only the stars and winds would take them. Columbus and his crew were exhausted, weary sea travelers wondering if they would ever see or feel the soles of their feet touch dry land ever again. When in what must have been an answer to many prayers, they came upon the small island that crossed their ship's path unexpectedly. Imagine the joy those sailors must have felt from their dangerous voyage ending in one way but just beginning in many others, not by falling off the edge of the earth but with the new discovery they had set out to find.

Christening the island of San Salvador (Christ the savior.) The most beautiful land eyes have ever seen as Columbus described it. San Salvador is a small island of the southeast Bahamas 10 miles long by 4 miles wide. The odds of Columbus coming across this beautiful but small area of land in a vast sea were less likely than man landing on the moon centuries later. Much of San Salvador is uninhabitable. The primary form of transportation is a golf cart to go around the one lane road circling the island, which has no stop signs. Locked in by fresh water lakes it is the tip of a submerged underwater mountain, with the clearest most diverse sparkling waters found anywhere on earth. Scuba divers the world over come to dive its deep underwater cliffs, called wall diving. The steep 15,000 foot drop just yards off the beach gives the water an intense purple shimmer usually seen only in the deepest depths in middle of the ocean where the closest land is thousands of miles away. Known as a place where giant winter wahoos gather, its allure beckoned for years, making its call impossible to be left unanswered. Getting there would be an adventure in itself. The fun of which more than made the discomfort worth the sacrifice. Of course for any real sailor, island hopping had to be the only way to go. Traveling by plane will get you there faster but leaving modern conveniences behind in favor of more rustic modes of transportation lets you take in the charms of the scenery in ways that are missed with more direct travel, making you feel like a native. Crossing from Florida by ferry to Abaco, an island in the northern Bahamas, was the first leg of the trip as well as its most comfortable. Arriving into port on the tourist side of Abaco, its beaches lined with high rise hotels, and casinos, with a distinct modern feel our destination to the island's other more-primitive side where we were to meet up with our buddy Keith, and by now much to no one's surprise who knew him word of his heroic crossing was circulating around the island. Next it required hopping on a van for the 35 mile trek on a bumpy one lane dirt road. Keith, who was safely tucked away in a sea shack in a Cay (Key) called Lubbers' quarters, had spent the days scuba diving. We had hoped to fish on his now seaworthy proven catamaran before moving onto the next leg of the trip. The winds were blowing steadily, the forecast predicting a break would not be coming for at least a week. Not being familiar with the waters where the honey holes (areas holding fish) were. We tried going out one day, staying out for half a day before deciding to come back. Keith's catamaran took on the waves differently than the V Hulls; we were used to having less fiberglass for the water to pound against meant more space for the waves to move through unimpeded underneath the catamarans middle, lessening the bounce giving stiff joints and knees some temporary relief. Coming in early gave us a lot of time to share fish stories. Ah! What about the Blue Marlin from last year that tail danced for one hundred yards before coming off the line.? Yeah, I remember that one. Pulling lures 50 miles from land about to pass a crate we found floating in the water behind the boat. Captain Mike uttered, "here she comes now," the words barely out of his mouth when a big blue marlin that must have easily been a grander (1,000 lbs.) Exploded out of the water, face and broad shoulders turning away from the boat in a run so powerful I have felt it in my bones from that moment forever forward. The grand marlin attacked the lure and ran with a purposeful fury unlike anything I have ever experienced before or since. Teasing us when she got up on her tail, moonwalking across the water before spitting the hook. I have often wondered what might have happened if instead of the heavier lure we were using if the giant marlin had struck a lighter weight cedar plug. Cedar plugs had always worked for me, they worked for tuna, wahoo, and marlin. On a troll they leave a trail of bubbles in their wake that attracts fish. When hooked the lighter weight gives the fish less resistance to leverage against. When I think back on that mighty marlin, besides the feeling I get in my bones, I think of the magnificence of the mighty creatures our Lord has put here on this earth.

 We had landed several other blues before, but none ever came close to giving us the thrill that one did, in a show of man vs beast. That marlin was all beast. Bob Sr. landed a blue marlin by himself in a standing upright position on the stern once. Not realizing the fish took a run reappearing when he made a leap several hundred yards in front of the bow. Another one pounced on a lure called a "teardrop" at 9:30 AM, probably a male. Females in the ocean always seemed to act feistier....But it's the one that came out from behind the pallet with indescribable force that will always make me pause, standing in awe. We each ordered a salad at the local market that seemed to as Keith said "reproduce on itself" the more it was eaten. On the next leg we needed to catch another ferry to Nassau. Still a few hundred miles away, the last leg of the excursion would take us from Nassau to the beautiful remote island of San Salvador. Being there felt like another world. A new world just the way Columbus found it. Where time marches forward but in a spiritual way remains at a standstill. We had caught a lot of wahoos off of Destin, finding them on weed lines or floating objects such as trees, or pallets where we once found a school of them. The biggest one not counting the 100 lb fish Bob Jr. had on the line was an 82 pounder caught on a troll. The ones we were after in San Salvador seemed to be another species altogether. In the Bahamas, wahoos under 80 lbs were called snakes. They tasted good and the islanders loved them, but the 100 lb monsters were the ones that made great conversation pieces. The islanders also loved the barracuda that would often eat up the rigged ballyhoo dressed with a skirt they used as bait. They did not seem the least bit concerned with the possibility of contracting ciguatera poisoning. If ingested, ciguatera, a bacteria that lives on ocean reefs carried then spread by reef fish who eat them, could make humans very sick and in very severe cases be even worse. Deep water so close to shore made looking for signs of fish unnecessary. We knew where to look for them. Start out deep in the purple water working your way in. We caught a few snakes in the 50 lb range but not the big one we sought after. Settling for seeing one hung at the dock from another boat would have to do. And that was thrilling enough. We had seen sea turtles, an oceanic whitetip shark, one of the more aggressive species of shark, but the catch of the trip came as a complete surprise when from the depths of the deep water lure we were trolling a 50lb mahi-mahi devoured the underwater lure we offered. A lesson learned that it pays off not only placing the right bait in the water but also placing the right bait at the right depth. We learned this same lesson many years earlier in Key Largo with three red snappers and a big bull dolphin in Islamorada. Bob Jr. had been the lucky one on this day. As a twelve year old catching three red snappers by letting out enough line to get deep enough to find them. Three hundred feet, about 100 feet deeper than the more common depth of 200 where they are usually found. He was the only one on the boat who caught any fish. Back in Destin Drawbridge was getting "Skunked" one day. He was captain on another boat catching nothing by mid afternoon. He pulled up to us assuming the bite had been slow for every boat he was talking about heading back in for the day. From the top of his boats bridge tower. Drawbridge asked us how the bite had been going. Playing it cool, ho hum & a bottle of rum, we told Drawbridge the reason he wasn't catching any fish was because the boat he was captain of was named "Captain Kidd." Boats named after Pirates were jinxed, superstition had it, if a captain of any ship or boat named after pirate got "skunked," the captain would be forced to walk the plank by sundown. Not yet ready to show off our good fortune, we kept Drawbridge in suspense before showing him our catch. Finally we opened our cooler, letting Drawbridge have a look in. Much to his surprise and possibly dismay the cooler was loaded with groupers of all kinds. Gag, Scamp, Yellowfin, Red, Yellowtail, Warsaw, Strawberry, Snowy and some Almaco Jack's. Instead of heading back in, proud fisherman he was, Drawbridge said the gauntlet had been thrown down, accepted the challenge. No way he would be going back "skunked" for the day. Drawbridge throttled his engines, then headed out keeping his baits in the water. He knew if a fisherman can fight through the frustration that happens to all fisherman, the rewards will come eventually. The Islamorada bull took off on a pitched bait, almost taking the light spinning rod we were using with him. The spinning rod is by far the most challenging way of catching mahi. Twenty pound test line with plenty of loose drag enabling the fish to make his runs makes for a great championship fight. The challenge being only second only to the fun it provides. Making incredible leaps the mahi bull took off with bursts of energy that sent shockwaves through my fingertips, making endless runs before succumbing. Forty-seven pounds of what felt like pure muscle was his official weight. He had enough meat on his bones to feed a party of six. Locals call it "Rinde Mucho," meaning it goes a long way. We had the mahi prepared at a seafood restaurant where they used five different recipes, each one as delicious as the next, my favorite being blackened, giving the taste just enough of a touch of spice. Everyone enjoyed the meal. In seaman's jargon, the term "Potato Head" is used to describe rough waves seen on the horizon while standing safely on firm dry land looking out over the sea. Where the term comes from is unknown but fits perfectly. When the wind direction blows against the current it creates an upswell in the wave, turning the wave into what looks like the shape of a potato. Thicker on the bottom with a curved slender pointed head the curvature of the wave looking like hair growing out at the top. On very rough days they look like rows of potato heads against the backdrop of the horizon where the water meets the sky. The aroma of the sea salt still tickling the senses. There weren't any "Potato Heads" to be seen on the water that day, only Islamorada's cloudless clear blue sky and the frigate birds diving straight into the water, alerting us to where the fish were. The mahi was accompanied on the table by a big side of as I liked to say of baked "Potato Heads." In San Salvador there was a little reminder of the USA when in the sky above us two military aircraft were spotted flying overhead. Probably on patrol duty. Not knowing in the Gulf of Mexico on a future trip U.S. Air Force planes would help us find some long weed lines. Passing us overhead in a circular motion several times until we realized they were trying to tell us something. We had been fishing a few short miles away from where they could see up above from the friendly skies lay a long wide weed line undetected by our radar. Our sense of wonder of what we might find turned to satisfaction when we realized the weedline was holding wahoo and mahi. We all got up on the bridge waving to them on their final pass. Knowing they were as much a part of the catch as we were. We hope they saw us wave or better as they flew away, losing us in the clear blue sky. We hope they saw us salute!!

A FLICKER IN THE WATER

Destin discovering a new world!

BOB GONZALEZ

One of the three ships Christopher Colombus sailed to the new world. The Santa Maria was the largest and also the slowest of the ships. It took five weeks to sail across the Atlantic from the Canary Islands before stumbling onto San Salvador, Bahamas. The Santa Maria was used mainly for cargo and sailed with 18 men on board, including Columbus himself. She eventually sank after hitting a reef off the coast of Haiti. The ship's wood was then used to build a fort on land. The other two ships were named Nina and the Pinta. They each carried 26 sailors. The Pinta was the fastest of the three ships, reaching a top speed of 8 knots and is believed to be the first ship to spot the island of San Salvador. The Santa Maria reached top speed at 4 knots and could not go near the coastline because of its deep draft. The Nina was by far Columbus's favorite ship, and he continued to use her on subsequent voyages.

Blue Marlin: this one is probably a male, biting a lure at 9:30 AM: Gary, Bob Jr. and Captain Mike. Bob Jr. holding the fish up by the mid section to ease the curvature on the spine while at the same time supporting its organs. After the picture, we released him to fight another day.

BOB GONZALEZ

This one, probably a female, left a lasting impression on my soul, the image of which I can never forget. Its powerful explosion out from under the water a bite so strong and a run so furious it's resonance still reverberates throughout my body.

A FLICKER IN THE WATER

What is that song? "Never can say goodbye" No No No Ohh!

BOB GONZALEZ

A salute to our troops, especially the coast guard who are there day and night patrolling the seas. Semper paratus (Always ready).

POETIC FISHING LICENSE

Being good stewards is what's been asked by our CREATOR: The earthly seas bountiful GENERATOR: Fishing and poetry go hand in HAND: One written deep in the depths of the wet ocean water far from the beach's crystalline SAND: The other on the shore of solid footed dry LAND: The best months being April through JUNE: So make sure to book your trip SOON: This wahoo was caught a little after NOON: Sometimes they can be caught under the starry sky of the big blue MOON: You can usually find them best in the early morning light where the baitfish CONGREGATE: If you don't arrive on time, it will probably be too LATE: So if you want to catch the big one of your dreams sleep, set your alarm clock early, there's no need to HESITATE: Bon appetito, they are great with a little lemon on the DISH: Wahoo are as fun to catch as they are to taste, for all adventurers who love to FISH:

BOB GONZALEZ

FOREWORD FROM FIRST MATE VINNI GARCIA

Fishing is a helluva drug! It is a passion of love and a symbol of friendship and prosperity. Making memories, bonding, and relaxation are some of the benefits of the act. A successful trip is not about what you catch but the experience and what you have gained from it. The success of my many trips have very little to do with the fishing, and the fish on my board are little indication of my deckhand availability and skills. I just tie good knots and give anglers good advice while coaching anglers to success. I can take complete non-fishermen and turn them into astute bottom fishers, and I take experienced fishermen and improve their abilities, and I never have issues with people who won't listen, because I know how to identify a closed mind (I just find a subtle, effective and suitable way to teach) and handle it accordingly. I have taken many fishermen (and women) on charter boats, private boats, and party boats since 1993. I have enjoyed them all and learned from every single person, their stories and most of all what makes them laugh. Some of my best memories were on the Twister with Captain Mike, Bob Sr. and Bob Jr. All three of them were top notch fishermen, and I most enjoyed the friendly rivalries between them. Through all the ribbing at the end of the day, it didn't really matter who caught the most or the biggest fish. We all had fun just being a part of the team. I am a very astute/attentive fisherman (means I am constantly learning and evolving), but my greatest gift is being sensitive to the slightest detail of what my customers need and want out of their fishing trip (and mate), also in making people laugh. It is the greatest feeling to bring others joy through the very thing that brings me joy. Fishing. One day I am going to put all my memoirs into a book and only after my ashes are scattered in the Gulf of Mexico will it be read....

A FLICKER IN THE WATER

First Mate Vinni Garcia with a 72 pound gag grouper caught in from Destin in 2017. The world record gag is 80 pounds 6 ounces also caught from Destin in 1993.

BOB GONZALEZ

Fishing has long been a lifeblood for mankind and one of its noblest pursuits since the beginning of time. This is Jesus with his disciples after telling them to lower their nets. More of the story is in the acknowledgements below.

ACKNOWLEDGEMENTS

"Master" Simon replied, "we have fished all night and caught nothing." But if you say so I'll let down the nets." Every fisherman at one time or another will understand the frustration Simon was expressing after fishing all night in the sea of Galilee without any luck. The sea of Galilee is actually a landlocked freshwater lake in northern Israel. I had always believed it was part of a saltwater body. "Go out into the deep water and let your nets down," Jesus said to them. So many fish were brought up on that last drop the nets could not hold all the fish. Every dedicated fisherman can also understand the good fortune that awaits them if they persist long enough. The battle is never over unless you quit. It is in this spirit I want to acknowledge all the people who contributed directly or indirectly to this book. My parents, Bob Sr. whom you got to know a little bit in the book. My mother, Idalia (Dolly) from the island of Puerto Rico another tropical fisherman's paradise, who continues to inspire us everyday. Without them none of these stories would have been made possible. Drawbridge, may you be resting peacefully fishing on heaven's oceans. Someday we will all join you and be able to gather again in search of that one tuna who inspired the creation of "A FLICKER IN THE WATER." The crew and all who fished with us aboard the Twister, the memories we made together will outlast us all. Thank for sharing your knowledge and love of fishing. Mariel Hemingway, granddaughter of Ernest Hemingway whose book "Old Man and the Sea" continues to stir the passions of all of us who love our oceans. Thank you Mariel for lending us your name and supportive commentary about my book. It is a true honor!

CPSIA information can be obtained
at www.ICGtesting.com
Printed in the USA
BVHW022346240622
640558BV00004BA/11